The Myth of the Generational Curse

G. A. N. James

Copyright © 2007 by G. A. N. James

The Myth of the Generational Curse
by G. A. N. James

Printed in the United States of America

ISBN 978-1-60477-292-0

All rights reserved solely by the author. The author guarantees all contents are original and do not infringe upon the legal rights of any other person or work. No part of this book may be reproduced in any form without the permission of the author. The views expressed in this book are not necessarily those of the publisher.

Unless otherwise indicated, Bible quotations are taken from the New King James Version. Copyright © 1982 by Thomas Nelson, Inc.

www.xulonpress.com

Contents

Introduction ix
1. Occultism 13
2. Blessing and Cursing 23
3. Prosperity Gospel 31
4. What Is the Generational Curse? 37
5. Do Scriptures Support the
   Generational Curse Doctrine? 43
6. God Rejects the Idea of Generational Curse 51
7. Removal of the Curse of Sin 59
8. The Generational Blessing 63
9. The Genealogy of Jesus Christ 69
10. Blessed in Christ 77
11. Dip Your Buckets Where You Are 87
12. The Generational Curse Doctrine Is a Myth 91

Foreword

I sincerely say this to everyone who will read this book. Do not seek for the authorization or authentication of the truth of the message of this book from who I am. I consider myself to be nothing without God or what God has made me to be. I consider my words or my opinion absolutely meaningless and vain outside of the truth of the Word of God. Therefore, as you read this book, I urge you to seek for the authorization and authentication of the truth of the message of the book from the anointing or unction which the Holy Spirit gives to every believer in Christ. I have carefully based every statement of the message of this book, not on my own speculations or assumptions, but on Scripture passages from the Bible, which I believe to be the Word of God. Therefore I urge you, dear reader, to read those Scripture passages referred to in the book and let the Spirit reveal to you personally the truth they convey. If the truth the Holy Spirit reveals to you from these Scripture passages confirms the message of this book, then agree with the Word of God and not merely with me. If the truth the Holy Spirit of God reveals to you from these Scripture passages is not consistent with the message of the book, then reject the book and the message I convey in it. God bless you.

The Author

Introduction

Solomon once referred to the little foxes that spoil the vine (Song 2:15). What intrigues me about this statement is its implication for the potential destructiveness by certain things which may appear insignificant but are cunning and dangerous and can wreak extreme havoc. Time and again the adversary the devil has introduced little foxes in the Lord's vineyard. They appear in the forms of insignificant doctrines and practices but are cunningly designed to attack the fundamental truths of the Christian faith.

The myth of the generational curse doctrine is one such little fox. It may seem to be an insignificant doctrine, but when closely examined in the light of the Word of God, it attacks the very foundation of the Christian faith. By proposing that believers in Christ may be affected by generational curses, which can only be effectively removed by the exorcising prayers of certain ministers, it cunningly attacks the foundation of the Christian faith.

Fundamental to the Christian faith is complete belief in and absolute dependence on the thorough effectiveness of the cross of Christ and the shed blood of Christ to atone for and free man from all sins and the guilt and judgments of sin. Any doctrine or practice that proposes that the atoning work of Christ is not fully adequate by itself and prescribes alternative or additional procedures to free man from sin or any form of the judgments of sin is an affront to the cross of Christ. There is no other method given under heaven to save man from sin and the curse of sin but faith in Christ and the atoning work of the cross of Christ.

For a fact, the Scriptures warn us of the disastrous consequences of despising the effectiveness of the atoning work of Christ and seeking after alternative or additional rituals or procedures to free us from the power and judgments of sin. We are warned in Hebrews 10:26-29: "For if we sin wilfully after we have received the knowledge of the truth, there no longer remains a sacrifice for sins, but a certain fearful expectation of judgment, and fiery indignation which will devour the adversaries. Anyone who has rejected Moses' law dies without mercy on the testimony of two or three witnesses. *Of how much worse punishment, do you suppose, will he be thought worthy who has trampled the Son of God underfoot, counted the blood of the covenant by which he was sanctified a common thing, and insulted the Spirit of grace?"*

This book titled *The Myth of the Generational Curse* is intended to expose and dispel the myth of the misleading doctrine of the generational curse and to show the doctrine has no foundation in the Word of God. The study notes that, whereas the Bible refers to the curse of sin or the curse of the Law, which has affected all mankind from generation to generation because all have sinned, there is no support in the Bible for a so-called generational curse which is supposed to be inherited by certain families from their ancestors. It concludes by showing the misleading generational curse doctrine is an affront to God's character of mercy, grace and divine justice and is denounced by God. Moreover Christ, through His atoning work on Calvary, has redeemed all who believe in Him from the universal curse of sin, and therefore the blessing of God is upon all believers in Christ of every nation.

In the book's examination of the generational curse doctrine, believers in Christ are brought to the awareness of their irreversible blessedness in Christ. The study presents powerful Scripture passages which awaken the believer to the profound truth of being blessed of God in Christ with all spiritual blessings and, hence, to the fact that a believer in Christ cannot be affected by any curse. Christian believers are urged to recognize the truth of their blessedness in Christ and free their minds from the bondage of fear generated by the false idea of a generational curse affecting them.

The study in no way denies the reality that believers in Christ are constantly opposed by the forces of evil and darkness. But it highlights the truth that God has delivered us from the power of darkness and evil and has translated us into the kingdom of His dear Son, through whom we are made to be more than conquerors as we wrestle against principalities, against powers, against the rulers of the darkness of this age, against spiritual hosts of wickedness in the heavenly places. In other words, believers in Christ face the opposing forces of darkness and evil already fully equipped by God to be always triumphant through Christ (Ephesians 6:10-18; 2 Corinthians 2:14; Romans 8:37).

The aim of this study is to debunk the myth of the generational curse doctrine by highlighting the wonderful truths of deliverance, peace and blessedness, which the message of the gospel presents to all who believe in Christ. This study will inspire faith, peace and security in the hearts and minds of believers who may have been tormented by the fear of being under a curse as a result of accepting as truth the deceitful lies contained in the myth of the generational curse doctrine.

The study deals with the subject of the myth of the generational curse under twelve revealing topics: (1) Occultism; (2) Blessing and Cursing; (3) The Prosperity Gospel; (4) What Is the Generational Curse Doctrine; (5) Do the Scriptures Support the Generational Curse Doctrine; (6) God's Rejection of the Idea of Generational Curse; (7) The Removal of the Curse of Sin; (8) The Generational Blessing; (9) Genealogy of Jesus Christ; (10) Blessed in Christ; (11) Dip Your Buckets Where You Are; and, in conclusion, (12) The Generational Curse Doctrine Is a Myth.

1. Occultism

Growing Interest

❖ *Interest in occultism seems to have impacted every institution in society.*

There is an unprecedented growing interest in the occult in society today. Political, judicial, economic, commercial, educational, family and religious institutions—every social institution—seem to be in some form or other showing interest, if not involved, in the occult. People of every class and status are turning to their so-called psychics seeking blessings for themselves and curses for their enemies. This interest in occultism seems to have impacted every institution in society.

The popularity of these kinds of superstitious beliefs and practices has given a significant measure of sophistication to what essentially is nothing other than modern-day sorcery or witchcraft. Obviously such interest has seeped into the Christian religion giving rise to questionable practices and beliefs which are deceiving many.

Believers must be warned to be extremely careful. This popular surge of interest in occultism, in its various forms such as pseudo-scientism, Rosicrucian, mythology, astrology, psychic practices, divination, witchcraft, voodoo or obeah, and the like, has been perverting the Christian religion mainly through the influence of the pseudo-religious movement called the New Age movement.

Isaiah's warning of the deceitfulness and disastrous consequences of seeking for counsel by occultist means instead of looking to the Word of the Lord is still relevant today. "And when they say to you, 'Seek those who are mediums and wizards, who whisper and mutter,' should not a people seek their God? Should they seek the dead on behalf of the living? To the law and to the testimony! If they do not speak according to this word, it is because there is no light in them. They will pass through it hard-pressed and hungry; and it shall happen, when they are hungry, that they will be enraged and curse their king and their God, and look upward. Then they will look to the earth, and see trouble and darkness, gloom of anguish; and they will be driven into darkness (Isaiah 8:19-22).

The New Age Movement

The New Age movement is a subtle undefined movement which seems to be a concoction of a corrupt combination of humanism, science, psychic practices and all sorts of vain religious and diabolic beliefs and practices. New Age teachings have infiltrated into the Christian religion introducing superstitious ideas and practices that have absolutely no foundation in the Holy Scriptures.

Christian believers, more than ever before, need to be careful of the teachings they accept and must search the Holy Scriptures with the unction of the Holy Spirit for a proper understanding of the Word of God. Some of these distorted teachings are becoming very popular, but Christian believers should realize that the popularity of a religious teaching or practice in no way means it is necessarily based on divine truth.

Many Christian believers neglect to search the Scriptures for themselves and to seek for divine revelation from the Holy Ghost to discern the things which are of God. As a result, many have become easily carried away by various kinds of doctrines of men and devils. These are they who become easily ensnared by the New Age movement, which accepts and promotes everything which appears religious without distinction between truths and falsehood, or good and evil.

For instance, a very popular request by some Christians today is for what they call "a word." They will not seek God diligently and study the Scriptures to know the will of God, especially when they must make important decisions in their lives; but they are anxiously asking for "a word" — and usually these words they want are of the sort that tickle their itching ears and feed their superstitious minds.

Sometimes, even if these so-called words are fancifully far out from the basic truths of the Scriptures, they will be naively accepted as of God by some weak-minded people, especially if they are uttered by self-styled prophets who themselves, like the prophet Balaam, will say or pray anything only for the pay.

Occultist Pretensions

❖ *The biggest challenge for Christians arises when occultists operate in the guise of the Christian religion.*

There are many false prophets operating in the midst of God's people and are deceiving many with their occultist pretensions. Attempts by occultist practitioners to associate themselves with God's people are not just a modern phenomenon. The Bible gives several accounts of such pretentious occultist attempts and how they were brought down by the power of God.

For instance, we read one of the dramatic accounts of the contests between Pharaoh's sorcerers and Aaron in Exodus 7:8-12: "Then the Lord spoke to Moses and Aaron, saying, 'When Pharaoh speaks to you, saying, 'Show a miracle for yourselves,' then you shall say to Aaron, 'Take your rod and cast it before Pharaoh, and let it become a serpent.' So Moses and Aaron went in to Pharaoh, and they did so, just as the Lord commanded. And Aaron cast down his rod before Pharaoh and before his servants, and it became a serpent. But Pharaoh also called the wise men and the sorcerers; so the magicians of Egypt, they also did in like manner with their enchantments. Every man threw down his rod, and they became serpents. *But Aaron's rod swallowed up their rods.*" Several other attempts by Pharaoh's sorcerers and magicians to contest with Aaron and Moses were defeated (Exodus 9).

Another classical example is that of the woman with the spirit of divination and her attempt to associate herself with Paul and his missionary team in the city of Thyatira. She pretended to adulate them with her divination that they were servants of the Most High God.

We read the account in Acts 16:16-18: "Now it happened, as we went to prayer, that a certain slave girl possessed with a spirit of divination met us, who brought her masters much profit by fortune-telling. This girl followed Paul and us, and cried out, saying, 'These men are the servants of the Most High God, who proclaim to us the way of salvation.' And this she did for many days. But Paul, greatly annoyed, turned and said to the spirit, 'I command you in the name of Jesus Christ to come out of her.' And he came out that very hour." The woman was saying nothing wrong about Paul, and Paul could have easily accepted her divination if he did not have the ability to discern the occultist spirit with which she spoke.

Not everyone who gives you 'a word' which seems correct is doing it by the Spirit of God.

A final example is the interesting account of the Jewish chief priest's sons who tried to imitate Paul by casting out demons. We read in Acts 19:11-16: "Now God worked unusual miracles by the hands of Paul, so that even handkerchiefs or aprons were brought from his body to the sick, and the diseases left them and the evil spirits went out of them. Then some of the itinerant Jewish exorcists took it upon themselves to call the name of the Lord Jesus over those who had evil spirits, saying, 'We exorcise you by the Jesus whom Paul preaches.' Also there were seven sons of Sceva, a Jewish chief priest, who did so. And the evil spirit answered and said, 'Jesus I know, and Paul I know; but who are you?' Then the man in whom the evil spirit was leaped on them, overpowered them, and prevailed against them, so that they fled out of that house naked and wounded."

The biggest challenge for Christians is when occultists operate in the guise of the Christian religion. John advises us in 1 John 4:1: "Beloved, do not believe every spirit, but test the spirits, whether they are of God; because many false prophets have gone out into the world." Occultists operating like ministers of God are still very active in these days. Believers in Christ must be on the lookout for these deceivers. God has given to His children the gift of discerning spirits to identify these pretenders and expose them.

Overcoming Occultism

❖ *The Bible makes it clear that those who practice or participate in occultism are weakened and subdued before those who trust in God.*

Occultism with its ideas of superstition and sorcery has its origin in heathenism or pagan culture. This is brought out quite clearly in God's instructions regarding these practices to the children of Israel when they were preparing to enter the Promised Land.

In Deuteronomy 18:9-14, Moses instructed the children of Israel as follows: "When you come into the land which the Lord your God is giving you, you shall not learn to follow the abominations of those nations. There shall not be found among you anyone who makes his son or his daughter pass through the fire, or one who practices witchcraft, or a soothsayer, or one who interprets omens, or a sorcerer, or one who conjures spells, or a medium, or a spiritist, or one who calls up the dead. For all who do these things are an abomination to the Lord, and because of these abominations the Lord your God drives them out from before you. You shall be blameless before the Lord your God. For these nations which you will dispossess listened to soothsayers and diviners; but as for you, the Lord your God has not appointed such for you."

The various practices which are mentioned in this Scripture passage—for instance, one who practices witchcraft, or a soothsayer, or one who interprets omens, or a sorcerer, or one who conjures spells, or a medium, or a spiritist, or one who calls up the dead—are actually what are modern-day psychic practices, spiritism and obeah. In fact, the generational curse concept is linked to modern-day spiritism, based on the pagan concept and beliefs in the worship of the spirits of ancestors, the transmission of the spirits of ancestors to descendants, and reincarnation. These things are all derived from illusions and deceptions. The Bible declares categorically that these beliefs and practices are an abomination to the Lord and God's people should have no part in them.

What must also be noted in this Scripture passage is Moses' indication to the children of Israel that "because of these abominations the Lord your God drives them out from before you." Hallelujah! This indeed is an inspiration to the faith of God's people who refuse to participate in occultist practices but trust the Lord to fight their battles and supply their needs.

There are those who propagate and seem to magnify the power of witchcraft and tend to make even Christians feel so vulnerable and helpless before those who practice these abominations. Here the Bible, on the other hand, makes it clear that the practice of occultism weakened the inhabitants of Canaan and made them flee before the people of God. Thus those who practice or participate in occultism are weakened and subdued before those who trust in God.

Authority over Devils

❖ *Neither Satan, demons nor their human agents have any authority or power over believers in Christ.*

In fact, the Bible affirms that even the devil flees before believers in Christ. We are admonished in James 4:7: "Therefore submit to God. Resist the devil, and he will flee from you." If we who are believers in Christ will take a firm stand on the Word of God and submit to the truth of the Word of God, we will be able to resist the devil and put him to flight. This is the crux of the message of this book.

God has given to His children the grace and power to be more than conquerors. Therefore, rather than our being intimidated and weakened before occultism and evil practices, we should uncover their weakness and lies and put them to flight by opposing them by the truth of the Word of God.

It is unfortunate that there are some professing Christians who are convinced that witchcraft can overpower them. If Christian believers will have faith in God and walk in the light of His Word, they will in no way be deceived into thinking any sort of witchcraft can affect them, as even some misguided preachers would have them believe. Instead they will know the truth is that God has empowered His people to put to flight all those who confront them with the practice of witchcraft in whatever forms.

There is no denying that the practices of the evil works of darkness are rampant universally. There are people who have given themselves over to the devil to work all manner of iniquity. Some relentlessly oppose the truth of the gospel like Elymas the sorcerer upon whom Paul was forced to pronounce blindness, renouncing him in no flattering terms: "O full of all deceit and all fraud, you son of the devil, you enemy of all righteousness, will you not cease perverting the straight ways of the Lord" (Acts 13:10)?

One thing to bear in mind: if these practices, which involve devils, appear to be effective in any way, they can affect only those who themselves are subjected to devils. Jesus Christ, the Son of God, was manifested to destroy the works of the devil and has disarmed principalities and powers of darkness (1 John 3:8; Colossians 2:15). God has delivered us from the power of darkness and has translated *us* into the kingdom of His dear Son (Colossians 1:13). In addition, He has given to believers in Christ the power and authority over the forces of evil.

Jesus declared before His departure from earth in Mark 16:17-18: "And these signs will follow those who believe: 'In My name they will cast out demons; they will speak with new tongues; they will take up serpents; and if they drink anything deadly, it will by no means hurt them; they will lay hands on the sick, and they will recover.'" Moreover, as already pointed out, the Scriptures also exhort believers in Christ in James 4:7: "Submit to God. Resist the devil and he will flee from you."

The truth is that neither Satan, demons nor their human agents have any authority or power over believers in Christ.

As already pointed out, the Bible declares that Jesus Christ has disarmed and rendered powerless the devil and all principalities and powers of evil. God's children are kept by God from the evil one (John 17:15). Any doctrine which magnifies the powers of the devil, demons and evil spirits is diabolical propaganda originating from the lies of the devil. Believers in Christ must be careful not to subscribe to this diabolical propaganda, knowing that the Lord Jesus Christ, who is our strength, has disarmed the devil and triumphed over principalities and powers.

Devil's Propaganda

> ❖ *With lies and illusions the devil seeks to promote himself and his cohorts of demons and evil spirits as having powers which they actually do not have.*

The adversary, the devil, being a chronic liar, uses wiles and illusions to promote himself on the earth. These wiles and illusions are meant to ascribe to the devil and his cohorts of demons and evil spirits powers they actually do not possess. The devil's propaganda may be found in much of the writings and teachings on demonology, which falsely promotes demons and evil spirits as powerful creatures against which Christian believers may sometimes be helpless.

As already mentioned, the greatest challenge to Christians in dealing with occultism is when occultists operate in the guise of the Christian religion. These are those whom Satan uses to promote his propaganda. God has His true and faithful ministers. Satan too commissions his ministers. The Bible warns us of those who subtly promote Satan's propaganda. And we need to take these warnings seriously to avoid being deceived by what may appear to be of God but is of the devil.

Paul declares in 2 Corinthians 11:13-15: "For such are false apostles, deceitful workers, transforming themselves into apostles of Christ. And no wonder! For Satan himself transforms himself into an angel of light. Therefore it is no great thing if his ministers also transform themselves into ministers of righteousness, whose end will be according to their works."

2. Blessing and Cursing

Superstition

❖ *Many Christians today are severely tormented by nothing else but the fear of being under some sort of curse.*

As we have pointed out, the prevailing trend of superstition and occultism has made inroads into the Christian religion. As a result, the concept of blessing and cursing has become perverted and distorted by occultism among many Christians today. In their quest for an explanation of their problems and misfortunes in this life, some Christians easily and naively accept occultist conclusions instead of the faith and inspiration which can be derived from the sound promises of the Word of God.

Many Christians today are severely tormented by nothing else but the fear of being under some sort of curse. Some are fighting their battles in church by invoking curses on others. At the same time, there are some preachers, pastors and priests who are busy playing seers and sorcerers in churches. With their so-called revelations or visions of different types of curses on people and who invoked these curses, they conjure up superstitious ideas which plunge unwary Christians into tormenting fear, suspicion and hatred. In the process, families are divided and neighbours are turned against neighbours because of suspicion that a neighbour or member of their family put a curse on them. These beliefs and practices are clearly not of the Spirit of God because the Spirit of God inspires faith in the believer and does not bring tormenting fear or raise false accusations.

Curses

❖ *God has given no human being the power and authority to do harm to another by cursing.*

A curse is considered to be an evil omen which has been invoked on a person. There are ideas and practices, even from ancient times, that are associated with the concept of a curse as being some evil omen or spell which is mystically cast upon someone to bring misfortune or calamity. Those who pronounce such curses or spells claim to engage the power of gods or other mystical forces, including the devil. It is understood that curses are not mere evil wishes but are believed to have inevitable adverse effects when they are pronounced.

Ancient religions and mythologies are filled with these ideas. Whereas the concept of a curse involves various sorts of bizarre rituals and practices, and those involved in them are often deeply convinced they are achieving their aims, in reality these exercises are vain. Actually the use of spells and curses is based on the belief that one is able to enlist and persuade gods and evil powers to carry out one's dictates. The fact is there is no God but the Lord, who is the supreme authority and power in the universe. Other gods are vanities, and all other powers there may be, including the devil, are subject to the Lord. *God has given no human being the power and authority to do harm to another in this way.*

But it is evident that from ancient to modern times there are people who continue to engage in the vain and superstitious rituals and practices of cursing and are usually convinced these superstitions are effective. To underscore the futility of the practice of cursing, however, our Lord commands His disciples not to give any significance to it or engage in it. "Bless those who curse you," Jesus said (Luke 6:28). Paul also commands: "Bless those who persecute you; bless and do not curse" (Romans 12:14). Of course, there are many who engage in those practices and are not themselves convinced of the effectiveness of such practices but practice them mainly to deceive others.

The Curse of Sin

❖ *The curse of sin or the curse of the Law referred to in the Scriptures is inherited by all of mankind, and not specific families, because of the fall.*

The Bible's reference to a concept of a curse is the divine judgment brought upon man by God as a result of man's rebellion against God. This is the curse of sin which is a direct consequence of the fall of man.

We read this in Genesis 3:16-19: "To the woman He said, 'I will greatly increase your sorrow and your conception. In pain you shall bear sons, and your desire shall be toward your husband, and he shall rule over you.' And to Adam He said, 'Because you have listened to the voice of your wife and have eaten of the tree, of which I commanded you, saying, 'You shall not eat of it!' The ground is cursed for your sake. In pain shall you eat of it all the days of your life! It shall also bring forth thorns and thistles to you and you shall eat the herb of the field. In the sweat of your face you shall eat bread until you return to the ground, for out of it you were taken. For dust you are, and to dust you shall return.'"

Wherever curses are pronounced in the Bible they have been pronounced as judgments by God upon transgressors. Therefore, curses when mentioned in the Scriptures are usually referring to the consequences of disobedience to God in the same manner that blessings are the consequences of obedience to God (Deuteronomy 28). There is actually nothing mystical or superstitious about the curse of sin, since in a true sense all mankind is originally born under the curse, which when rightly understood means being in a morally and spiritually depraved condition.

According to the Holy Scriptures, we were all "dead in trespasses and sins, in which [we] once walked according to the course of this world, according to the prince of the power of the air, the spirit who now works in the sons of disobedience, among whom we all once conducted ourselves in the lusts of our flesh, fulfilling the desires of the flesh and of the mind, and were by nature children of wrath" (Ephesians 3:1-3).

Therefore, in its true scriptural sense the curse is a universal phenomenon in that all of mankind has inherited the curse of sin—princes and paupers, rulers and slaves, educated and uneducated, rich and poor, of all nations and tribes. Hence, unlike the superstitious concept of the generational curse, the curse the Bible mentions is the universal curse of sin and not some sort of evil omen of misfortune invoked on or resting on certain selective individuals, generations or races.

Biblical Evidence

❖ *Cursing and blessing are in the hand of the almighty God.*

Is there any evidence in the Bible that the so-called black or white art of cursing when invoked by men against one another does work? Absolutely none! There is no account in the Bible of this sort of superstitious curse being effectively invoked by any individual upon another individual.

There are accounts in the Scriptures of attempts of this sort of superstitious practice of cursing, but there is no instance given of anyone being a victim of such a curse. There are at least two instances reported in the Bible when cursing was invoked, but these attempts were to no avail.

For instance, King Balak seemed to have been convinced that cursing would have worked against the Israelites; he hired a prophet called Balaam to curse the people of Israel for him, but it could not work (Numbers 22–24). Balaam was forced to acknowledge to King Balak that *no one could curse someone whom God did not*—whom God has blessed no man can curse. Thus, Balaam recognized that the practice of cursing, which was common among the cultures of pagan nations and which he himself had no doubt been practicing, was a fake and that no man had power or authority to curse anyone.

In another instance in the Bible, Satan had envied the integrity and prosperity of a righteous man called Job and had carefully considered ways of destroying him. But he disappointedly acknowledged to God he could not penetrate God's protective hedge around Job. Satan is reported as telling God in Job 1:10: "Have You not made a hedge around him, around his household, and around all that he has on every side? You have blessed the work of his hands, and his possessions have increased in the land." In other words, *Satan tried to curse Job but recognized he had absolutely no power or authority of his own to curse Job and that there was no curse he could have brought upon Job because God had blessed Job.*

God Is Always in Control

❖ *God Himself carefully measures and controls the trials we go through.*

In the story of Job we see that God gave Satan measured and controlled permission to afflict Job. This demonstrated that Satan in no way can afflict God's people according to his evil intent and whims without God Himself allowing it by adjusting for His own purpose the hedge of protection He has placed around His people.

The story of Job therefore is a source of profound insight into the mystery of the sufferings and trials of the people of God. It gives us comfort in appreciating the truth that neither Satan nor anyone else can afflict God's people without the Lord allowing it. And we know that whatever the Lord allows works out for the good, not the curse, of His people, who love Him and are called according to His purpose (Romans 8:28).

The Bible assures us that "no temptation has taken you but what is common to man; but God is faithful, who will not allow you to be tempted above what you are able, but with the temptation also will make a way to escape, so that you may be able to bear it" (1 Corinthians 10:13). This scriptural truth gives us tremendous insight into the fact that *God Himself carefully measures and controls the trials which we go through*. Moreover, it assures us that the trials God allows us to undergo are not unique to us but are common to all men.

The tendency of many when going through trials is to assume that the Lord has forsaken them and they are singled out from the rest of humanity to go through trials no one else has experienced. This is not so. The Lord never forsakes His children. For reasons known only fully to Him trials seem to be necessary experiences for all His children.

But the Lord assures us that the trials He allows us to go through are trials which are common to all humanity and that He remains in complete control and management of the trials we go through in order that we may be able to bear it. Therefore, our trials are ultimately under God's control and not mystical mischief at the whims and malice of those who dispense superstitious curses.

Deliverance from the Curse

❖ *Deliverance from the curse of sin requires no mystical or superstitious formula, but simple faith in Jesus and His redemptive work on the cross.*

While the Bible makes mention of the universal curse or judgment which befell all of mankind because of the fall of man, it also presents the good news of God's universal plan of deliverance from the curse. The Bible teaches that God by His wonderful grace in bringing salvation to mankind delivered us from the curse of sin.

The fact that Jesus became the Lamb of God to atone for and eradicate sin is the basis for the truth that "Christ redeemed us from the curse... so that the blessing of Abraham might be to the nations in Jesus Christ, and that we might receive the promise of the Spirit through faith" (Galatians 3:13-14).

This is good news for mankind. Why would anyone who presumes to be a preacher of the gospel not prefer to herald the wonderful truth that the blessing of Abraham is made available to all nations in Christ through faith, rather than propagate the myth that generational curses or any curses are upon believers in Christ and can only be removed by his prayer or some other religious procedures?

All who put their faith in Christ are freed from the judgment and condemnation of sin. There is absolutely "no condemnation to them who are in Christ Jesus" (Romans 8:1). Indeed, deliverance from the curse of sin, it must be noted, requires no mystical or superstitious formula but simple faith in Jesus and His redemptive work on the cross.

God in mercy, love and wisdom designed salvation's plan for mankind and has made it available to us freely and with all simplicity through faith in Christ. Let us not complicate it. Christ has redeemed us from the curse of sin and has bestowed upon us His abundant blessings. This is the only means of deliverance provided by God, according to Scriptures, for deliverance from the curse of sin.

3. Prosperity Gospel

Gospel of Mammon

> ❖ *The prosperity gospel may be easily interpreted as a philosophy for serving mammon presented in religious form.*

A notable error that has led to much misunderstanding of what are blessings and what are curses is the identification of the blessings of God with material wealth. In other words, it assumes that everyone who is wealthy is blessed. Evidence shows that some people who live very profane and ungodly lives are very rich, famous and even highly honoured in society according to the standards and value-systems of this world. But can their worldly fame and fortune be equated to God's blessing? Are they really blessed in the sight of God? Absolutely not!

Jeremiah declares God's perspective of the wealth of the wicked and their eventual punishment in Jeremiah 5:26-29. "For among My people are found wicked men; they lie in wait as one who sets snares; they set a trap; they catch men. As a cage is full of birds, so their houses are full of deceit. Therefore they have become great and grown rich. They have grown fat, they are sleek; yes, they surpass the deeds of the wicked; they do not plead the cause, the cause of the fatherless; yet they prosper, and the right of the needy they do not defend. Shall I not punish them for these things" says the Lord. "Shall I not avenge Myself on such a nation as this?"

The prosperity gospel may be easily interpreted as a philosophy for serving mammon presented in religious form. Mammon is the idolization of material wealth. The prosperity gospel is so-called because its message is almost completely engrossed with the quest for material wealth and the attainment of material prosperity. Hence, it is essentially a gospel of mammon.

According to our Lord Jesus Christ, mammon or materialism demands such total commitment that it is impossible for anyone to serve mammon and God loyally at the same time. "No one can serve two masters; for either he will hate the one and love the other, or else he will be loyal to the one and despise the other. *You cannot serve God and mammon*" (Matthew 6:24).

Serenity of Christianity

❖ *Believers in Christ can afford to be content and know they are blessed in whatsoever condition or situation they are in with the assurance that God will supply their needs.*

Jesus Christ presents in His teachings a way of life that is simple, serene and content. He taught us that God intends for His children to live on earth a life fully committed to the kingdom of God and the righteousness of God. This way of life will ensure that our earthly needs are well provided for by the Father without our lives being driven by materialism or the pursuit of material wealth. According to Jesus, the pervasive pursuit of material wealth is a pagan way of life and is not for the children of God. While we pursue fully the matters of the kingdom of God and His righteousness, our heavenly Father who knows all that we have need of in the earth will provide them for us (see Matthew 6:25-34).

Believers in Christ can afford to be content and know they are blessed in whatsoever condition or situation they are in with the assurance that God will supply their needs. They can experience the constant peaceful consciousness that they are always complete and lacking nothing in Christ. Thus, what they do not have at any point in time is what God has deemed unnecessary for them. "The young lions suffer want and hunger; but *those who seek the Lord lack no good thing*" (Psalm 34:10). "For the Lord God is a sun and shield; the Lord bestows favour and honour. *No good thing does he withhold from those who walk uprightly*" (Psalm 84:11).

Materialism

> ❖ *The prosperity gospel is based on a vain philosophy of materialism, which reduces the blessings of God to material gain or profit.*

Many professing Christians, driven by the message of the prosperity gospel, are being misguided into thinking that to attain material wealth is to attain true blessings and not to be wealthy is to be under a curse. And so people who relatively lack material wealth are frantically seeking mystics to rid them of misperceived curses.

By accepting this materialistic philosophy, many professing Christians are convinced they are to have always the most and the best of this world's goods and must never suffer adversities. Hence, their trials and tribulations are considered to be due to the scourge of some sort of curse on their lives, invoked upon them by those who hate them or inherited from their ancestors.

Clearly, the prosperity gospel ignores two divine truths laid down in the Bible. One is that even if a man gains the whole world and loses his own soul it profits him absolutely nothing, and the other is that truly great gain or profit is godliness with contentment (Matthew 16:26; 1 Timothy 6:6). In other words, a life without spirituality through salvation in Christ is an unprofitable life, and a life of true godliness and contentment in Christ is a truly profitable life.

The prosperity gospel is based on a vain philosophy of materialism which reduces the blessings of God to material gain or profit and conjures up discontentment and anxiety in its adherents. Many Christians have derived their superstitious concept of blessings and curses from this vulgar philosophy.

Nevertheless, the Bible declares in 1 Timothy 6:6-11: "Godliness with contentment is great gain. For we brought nothing into the world, and it is clear that we can carry nothing out. But having food and clothing, we will be content. But they who will be rich fall into temptation and a snare, and into many foolish and hurtful lusts which plunge men into destruction and perdition. For the love of money is a root of all evil, of which some having lusted after, they were seduced from the faith and pierced themselves through with many sorrows. But you, O man of God, flee these things and follow after righteousness, godliness, faith, love, patience, and meekness."

Moreover, as we already noted, trials and tribulations are not synonymous with curses and are the experiences of godly people. For, according to the Scriptures, "they that shall live godly in Christ Jesus shall suffer persecution" (2 Timothy 3:16). Yes, the Scriptures indicate that the godly in Christ shall suffer persecution.

In fact, contrary to being considered curses, persecutions are described as blessings in disguise to believers in Christ. This is made plain in the words of our Lord Jesus

Christ: "Blessed are those who are persecuted for righteousness' sake, for theirs is the kingdom of heaven. Blessed are you when they revile and persecute you, and say all kinds of evil against you falsely for My sake. Rejoice and be exceedingly glad, for great is your reward in heaven, for so they persecuted the prophets who were before you" (Matthew 5:10-12).

Godly Priority

> ❖ *We, who are children of God by faith in Christ, must carefully guard against the wiles of the devil to generate anxiety, fear and discontentment in our minds by stirring doubts in our hearts concerning our Father's faithfulness in providing for us.*

According to Jesus Christ, while godless people focus on pursuing material wealth, even at the expense of peaceful and godly principles, the children of God are called to focus on pursuing the kingdom of God and the righteousness of God. While we who are the children of God focus on the pursuit of the kingdom and righteousness of God, our heavenly Father, who knows we have need of material things, will provide us with all these things.

The well-known exhortation of our Lord to the children of God will be ever relevant in this world of greed, covetousness and materialism: "Therefore do not worry, saying, 'What shall we eat?' or 'What shall we drink?' or 'What shall we wear?' For after all these things the Gentiles seek. For your heavenly Father knows that you need all these things. But seek first the kingdom of God and His righteousness, and all these things shall be added to you" (Matthew 6:31-33).

Our Lord's exhortation in no way implies children of God must have no ambition in improving their welfare on earth. What it does imply is that children of God must give priority to the principles and precepts of the kingdom and righteousness of God at all times in their life pursuits. And God in turn will ensure that their material welfare is well taken care of.

Therefore, the earthly goals children of God pursue and succeed in will not be at the expense of godly principles. At the same time, God will always give to His children what is sufficient for them of this earth's goods.

The trick of the devil is to distort our perceptions of incidents of adversities in our lives in order to cause us to doubt that God has promised to make even adversities produce what is good for us. Nonetheless we can overcome through faith and count our blessings in every situation the Lord takes us through. If we are children of God, we must carefully guard against the wiles of the devil to generate anxiety, fear and discontentment in our minds by stirring doubts in our hearts concerning our Father's faithfulness in providing for us.

4. What Is the Generational Curse?

Misconceptions

❖ *The occultist doctrine, known as the generational curse, is nowhere taught in the Scriptures. It is, however, upheld by many in the Christian religion usually because of a misconception of certain Scriptures or the cunning manipulation of the Scriptures by self-serving preachers whose aim is to intimidate weak-minded people for gainful exploitation.*

We know that, according to the Scriptures, the fall of Adam into sin brought the curse of sin and death upon the entire human race and, as a result, every human being inherited by birth the corrupt and sinful nature of Adam. Romans 5:12 tells us: "Therefore, just as through one man sin entered into the world, and death through sin, and so death spread to all men, because all sinned."

There is no greater woe which could have befallen the human race than the fall. In that sense one can conclude that from Adam and Eve all human beings from generation to generation were born under the curse of sin. But God has provided full salvation from the curse of sin by the redemptive work of His Son, Jesus Christ.

But this is not actually the idea being upheld by those who propagate the so-called generational curse doctrine. The generational curse is considered to be a specific curse distinct from the general curse of sin. This generational curse is said to be a curse in the form of some evil omen which plagues an individual or a family as a result of some particular iniquity or sin committed by an ancestor. Clearly the doctrine is steeped in superstition and occultism.

Victims of generational curses are said to have no power over the evils that plague them. They are considered to be innocent and inescapable victims of their cursed fate. Their doom arises not from their own wrongdoing but out of the fact that someone in their past genealogy committed some sort of wickedness or might have even been innocently the victim of a curse for which they, as descendants of that cursed ancestor, must bear the pernicious consequences.

Usually the curse is thought to have been imposed on the ancestor by some sort of sorcery and is destined to be transmitted from generation to generation. It is believed that even Christians, though considered saved in Christ, may be victims of the so-called generational curses. Those who teach the generational curse idea usually pose as breakers of the curse if the victims will come to them for prayer.

This occultist generational curse doctrine is nowhere taught in the Scriptures. It is, however, upheld by many in the Christian religion usually because of a misconception of certain Scripture passages or because of the cunning manipulation of the Scriptures by self-serving preachers whose aim is to intimidate weak-minded people for gainful exploitation.

Heredity

❖ *The child of God who suffers from a hereditary illness has no scriptural basis to believe he is under a generational curse. Instead he can put his faith in the Lord who will glorify Himself through this illness, either by healing or by demonstrating the power of His grace to enable His children to endure and triumph in the midst of adversity and affliction.*

A dangerous fallacy of the generational curse concept is that curses are hereditary. Heredity is the passing or transmission of characteristics or traits from parents to offspring. This is a biological or natural phenomenon or process.

The study of genetics teaches that the individual is biologically inseparably bound to his ancestors by birth and heredity. In the same manner, however, he is also tied to his descendants. As a result, numerous heritable characteristics are transmitted physically from generation to generation. Heritable characteristics or traits consist of both sound and ill characteristics. Hence, offspring may inherit both healthy and unhealthy biological characteristics from their parents.

Advocates of the generational curse concept have erroneously regarded heredity as involving not only the transmission of physical traits but also the transmission of spiritual traits. From that perspective curses and evil spirits, though considered spiritual phenomena, may be transmitted from generation to generation. This belief is steeped in the pagan doctrine of reincarnation which holds that spirits are reproduced in a sequence of births in bodily forms.

People who suffer from hereditary illnesses are thought by those who believe in the myth of the generational curse to be victims of generational curses. Such a teaching is dangerously erroneous and unscriptural by holding that a curse, which is considered a spiritual phenomenon, can be transmitted genetically. In this case it is clearly taking an obviously physical problem and making it into a mysterious, evil omen because of superstition.

Our Lord Jesus Christ plainly rejected the idea of illness being the result of generational curse. We read in John 9:1-3: "And passing by, He saw a man who was blind from birth. And His disciples asked Him, saying, 'Master, who sinned, this man or his parents, that he was born blind?' Jesus answered, *'neither has this man nor his parents sinned, but that the works of God might be revealed in him.'"*

The child of God who suffers from a hereditary illness has no scriptural basis to believe he is under a generational curse. Instead he can put his faith in the Lord who will glorify Himself through this illness, either by healing or by demonstrating the power of His grace to enable His children to endure and triumph in the midst of adversity and affliction.

Misinterpretation of Scriptures

The manipulation of Scriptures to promote erroneous ideas is a practice as old as the Scriptures, and God's people have been admonished to guard against such deceptive teachings. These ideas may appear to appeal to Scriptures, but when examined closely the Holy Ghost exposes their falsehood.

Peter admonishes us about this prevailing problem in the midst of the children of God. "But there were also false prophets among the people, even as there will be false teachers among you, who will secretly bring in destructive heresies, even denying the Lord who bought them, and bring on themselves swift destruction. And many will follow their destructive ways, because of whom the way of truth will be blasphemed. By covetousness they will exploit you with deceptive words; for a long time their judgment has not been idle, and their destruction does not slumber" (2 Peter 2:1-3).

The first reference in the Bible to what seems to be a basis for a generational curse doctrine is in Exodus 20:4-5: "You shall not make for yourself an idol, or any likeness of what is in heaven above or on the earth beneath or in the water under the earth. You shall not worship them or serve them; for I, the Lord your God, am a jealous God, visiting the iniquity of the fathers on the children, on the third and the fourth generations of those who hate Me."

Later in Exodus 34:6-7 the same statement is mentioned when God revealed Himself to Moses. "Then the Lord passed by in front of him and proclaimed, 'The Lord, the Lord God, compassionate and gracious, slow to anger, and abounding in loving-kindness and truth; who keeps loving-kindness for thousands, who forgives iniquity, transgression and sin; yet He will by no means leave the guilty unpunished, visiting the iniquity of fathers on the children and on the grandchildren to the third and fourth generations.'"

The portion of these Scripture passages which some propose to be a scriptural basis for the doctrine of the generational curse is the statement in which God is said to visit "the iniquity of the fathers on the children, on the third and the fourth generations." Let us closely examine these Scripture passages and see if truly their meaning, as well as the context in which the statement appears, provides any real basis for scriptural support for the generational curse doctrine.

5. Do Scriptures Support the Generational Curse Doctrine?

Examining the Scriptures

❖ *To show that the Scriptures support the generational curse doctrine, one would need to assume God will judge or condemn the innocent or punish people for wrongs they are not guilty of.*

Let us closely examine the Scripture passage in Exodus 34:6-7, which gives a context for the statement of God "visiting the iniquity of the fathers on the children, on the third and the fourth generations of those who hate Me." This Scripture passage is important to our study because it deals with the character of God as revealed to Moses by God Himself. "Then the Lord passed by in front of him and proclaimed, 'The Lord, the Lord God, compassionate and gracious, slow to anger, and abounding in loving-kindness and truth; who keeps loving-kindness for thousands, who forgives iniquity, transgression and sin; yet He will by no means leave the guilty unpunished, visiting the iniquity of fathers on the children and on the grandchildren to the third and fourth generations.'"

To show that the Scriptures support the generational curse doctrine, one would need to assume God will judge or condemn the innocent or punish people for wrongs they are not guilty of. In other words, do the Scriptures show God holds innocent people accountable for the iniquities of their ancestors? Can one rightly infer this about God's dealings with mankind from these Scripture passages being referred to by supporters of the generational curse myth?

We see in this Scripture passage that the Lord first reveals Himself as "the Lord, the Lord God, compassionate and gracious, slow to anger, and abounding in loving-kindness and truth; who keeps loving-kindness for thousands, who forgives iniquity, transgression and sin." In other words, contrary to unjustly punishing the innocent, by His very nature or character the Lord extends mercy and forgiveness to the guilty that turn to Him in sorrow and repentance for their iniquities. Then the Scripture goes on to reveal that "yet He will by no means leave the guilty unpunished, visiting the iniquity of fathers on the children and on the grandchildren to the third and fourth generations."

What then is the Scripture implying by this latter statement? At first it seems to contradict the former statement in which God is described as "The Lord, the Lord God, compassionate and gracious, slow to anger, and abounding in loving-kindness and truth; who keeps loving-kindness for thousands, who forgives iniquity, transgression and sin."

Why would God declare He forgives iniquity and transgression and sin and at the same time state He will by no means leave the guilty unpunished, visiting the iniquity of fathers on the children and on the grandchildren to the third and fourth generations? On the surface there may appear to be a contradiction or inconsistency in God's dealings with sinners. But on closer examination what seemed to be an inconsistency vanishes.

The Forgiven and the Guilty

❖ *Contrary to the misleading perception that God punishes the innocent, the truth is there are always those who, though guilty of sins, turn to God for mercy and find His forgiveness and escape condemnation, while there are those who also guilty of sin reject God's offer of forgiveness and bring condemnation upon themselves.*

Two categories of people are dealt with in the Scripture passage—the forgiven and the guilty. The forgiven are those who humbly turn to God in repentance of their sins and accept forgiveness through God's compassion, grace and loving-kindness. They can be no longer considered guilty because they have repented and received God's forgiveness. The guilty then are obviously those who evidently continue in iniquity rather than repenting and receiving God's forgiveness.

It is, therefore, obvious that those who remain guilty before God are not the forgiven and justified believers in Christ, but unbelievers who reject Christ. These are the guilty ones who by no means will be left unpunished because they despise and reject God's mercy and forgiveness.

In fact, in Exodus 20:5-6, the Scriptures make it clear that God was referring to two kinds of people: those who reject or hate Him and those who love and obey Him. "For I Jehovah your God am a jealous God, visiting the iniquity of the fathers upon the sons to the third and fourth generation of *those that hate me,* and showing mercy to thousands of *those that love Me and keep My commandments."*

Every individual born upon the earth is given an opportunity to find forgiveness of sins and to love and serve God in righteousness and holiness by the grace of God: "For the grace of God that brings salvation has appeared to all men"

(Titus 2:11). Moreover, "the Lord is not slack concerning his promise, as some men count slackness; but is longsuffering to us-ward, not willing that any should perish, but that all should come to repentance" (2 Peter 3:9).

Every individual of any generation, however sinful and wicked the previous or contemporary generation might have been, can find grace to live a righteous life before God and does not have to partake in any judgments for the evil doings of a previous or contemporary generation. In the same way there are individuals who will reject God's grace and continue to walk in the evil ways of their ancestors, or their contemporaries, and must therefore face the judgments due to their own evil doings.

Jesus made this very clear to Nicodemus in John 3:17-19: "For God did not send His Son into the world to condemn the world, but so that the world might be saved through Him. He who believes on Him is not condemned, but he who does not believe is condemned already, because he has not believed in the name of the only begotten Son of God. *And this is the condemnation, that the Light has come into the world, and men loved darkness rather than the Light, because their deeds were evil.*"

So contrary to the misleading perception that God punishes the innocent, the truth is there are always those who, though guilty of sins, turn to God for mercy and find His forgiveness and escape condemnation. And there are those who, also guilty of sin, reject God's offer of forgiveness and bring condemnation upon themselves. Divine justice invariably provides forgiveness and cleansing for every sinner who repents and trusts in Christ. First John 1:9 states: "If we confess our sins, He is faithful and just to forgive us our sins, and to cleanse us from all unrighteousness."

Hence, we see that no man can be condemned according to divine justice for sins of which he was never guilty or of which he has found forgiveness from God. Therefore, the scriptural statement that God visits the iniquity of the fathers on the children, on the third and the fourth generations, categorically cannot imply that God imposes the punishment of guilty fathers on their innocent children, grandchildren and great grandchildren, up to the fourth generation of descendants. What may be the case is that descendants who adopt the evil traditions of their ancestors may face judgments which are similar to the judgments with which their ancestors were punished. It is the iniquity God judges and therefore not those who are not guilty of the iniquity.

Cultural Transmission

> ❖ *Every generation, as well as every individual of a generation, who adopts and practices iniquity according to the evil traditions of their ancestors has the option to seek God's forgiveness and escape condemnation or to reject God's forgiveness and suffer condemnation.*

Human society is a cultural entity in which sinful behaviour and wickedness may be culturally transmitted from generation to generation. Apart from the fallen, sinful nature which all human beings from generation to generation inherit from Adam, the generational transmission of evil behaviour is not due to any inevitable mystical phenomenon but is actually a cultural transmission of evil habits and practices from generation to generation. Individuals and groups adopt the ways or traditions of their ancestors.

No generation or individual under God's justice is made to bear innocently the judgments of the iniquity of previous generations. The Scriptures declare plainly that God holds every individual of every generation accountable for his own sins and not for the sins of his ancestors or generation. *But every generation, as well as every individual of a generation,* who adopts and practices iniquity according to the evil traditions of their ancestors has the option to seek God's forgiveness and escape condemnation or to reject God's forgiveness and suffer condemnation. Descendants are judged because they are thus guilty of practicing their ancestors' iniquities in their respective generations and not as innocent victims judged for their ancestors' iniquities.

It must be noted that descendants who practice their ancestors' iniquities received by cultural transmission are not inevitably or genetically bound to practice their ancestors' iniquities and be judged for it. They can turn to God and find deliverance and forgiveness and live righteous lives and will not come under condemnation or judgments for their ancestors' evil practices.

An Affront to God's Justice and Mercy

❖ *The myth of the generational curse doctrines is designed by the wiles of Satan to subtly set aside the efficacy of the cross of Christ to deliver us from the judgments of sin and bestow upon us the fullness of the blessings of God in Christ.*

The generational curse doctrine, by assuming God judges innocent descendants for the iniquities of their ancestors, is obviously an affront to the justice and mercy of God. Satan, the adversary of God and a liar by nature, will seek relentlessly to propagate a myth like that of the generational curse in order to distort the integrity of the justice of God toward mankind.

Believers in Christ must be on constant alert in the Spirit of truth to discern and renounce the wiles of the devil. Wiles refer to deception, cunningness or trickery meant to fool or trap. Clearly the myth of the generational curse doctrines is designed by the wiles of Satan to subtly set aside the efficacy of the cross of Christ to deliver us from the judgments of sin and bestow upon us the fullness of the blessings of God in Christ. But if we remain rooted and grounded in the truth of the gospel we will not be trapped by the wiles of Satan. The Bible exhorts us to "put on the whole armour of God so that you may be able to stand against the wiles of the devil" (Ephesians 6:11).

Therefore, the actual threat to the Christian faith is not the so-called generational curse, which the Bible proves to be a false notion, but the deceptiveness of the idea of a generational curse. The idea subtly seeks to undermine faith in the faithfulness and justice of God. It is on the basis of God's faithfulness and justice we may believe God through the atoning work of Christ has forgiven and justified us who are descendants of Adam's fallen race. Therefore the generational curse doctrine is obviously an affront to the mercy and justice of God.

6. God Rejects the Idea of Generational Curse

God's Objection

❖ *Scriptures indicate that God categorically and plainly forbids His people to uphold the idea of generational curse.*

According to the Scriptures, the concept or principle of a generational curse fundamentally contradicts God's justice. Interestingly there are Scripture passages in which God categorically and plainly forbids His people to uphold the idea of generational curse. Let us examine some of these Scripture passages.

First of all, under the Law of Moses, it was forbidden to hold one generation responsible for the sins of another generation. In expounding the Law to the people of Israel, Moses plainly stated the point which contradicts any concept of God approving a generational curse principle. We read in Deuteronomy 24:16: "The fathers shall not be put to death for the sons; *neither shall the sons be put to death for the fathers*. Every man shall be put to death for his own sin."

Therefore, fundamental to the Law which God gave to direct His people under the Old Covenant in their relationships with Him and with one another was the principle of personal accountability rather than a generational responsibility for one's behaviour. *Clearly, therefore, it is erroneous for people to be told they are suffering because of the sins of their ancestors and that to obtain deliverance from such a generational curse they must repent of and seek forgiveness for the sins of ancestors.* The generational curse concept is contrary to the order of God in dealing with sin. An individual is responsible before God only for his own sins.

Children's Teeth at Edge

❖ ***"As I live," declares the Lord God, "you are surely not going to use this proverb in Israel anymore."***

We read in Ezekiel 18:1-4, 20, 25-27, 30-31: "Then the word of the Lord came to me, saying, 'What do you mean by using this proverb concerning the land of Israel, saying, "The fathers eat the sour grapes, but the children's teeth are set on edge"? 'As I live,' declares the Lord God, 'you are surely not going to use this proverb in Israel anymore. Behold, all souls are Mine; the soul of the father as well as the soul of the son is Mine. The soul who sins will die. *The person who sins will die. The son will not bear the punishment for the father's iniquity, nor will the father bear the punishment for the son's iniquity; the righteousness of the righteous will be upon himself, and the wickedness of the wicked will be upon himself.* Yet you say, "The way of the Lord is not right." Hear now, O house of Israel! Is My way not right? Is it not your ways that are not right? When a righteous man turns away from his righteousness, commits iniquity and dies because of it, for his iniquity which he has committed he will die. Again, when a wicked man turns away from his wickedness which he has committed and practices justice and righteousness, he will save his life. Therefore I will judge you, O house of Israel, each according to his conduct,' declares the Lord God. 'Repent and turn away from all your transgressions, so that iniquity may not become a stumbling block to you. Cast away from you all your transgressions which you have committed and make yourselves a new heart and a new spirit! For why will you die, O house of Israel?'"

In this Scripture passage we see that the children of Israel were propagating a proverb: "the fathers eat the sour grapes, but the children's teeth are set on edge." Such a proverb clearly suggested belief in what is today known as the generational curse. They might have derived the proverb from pagan beliefs they had adopted. To God, however, this occultist proverb being propagated by His own people was a sinister affront to His justice. It meant the people were shamelessly advocating that 'the way of the Lord is not right.'

God's straightforward response to this was: *"As I live, you are surely not going to use this proverb in Israel anymore.* Behold, all souls are Mine; the soul of the father as well as the soul of the son is Mine. The soul who sins will die. The person who sins will die. *The son will not bear the punishment for the father's iniquity, nor will the father bear the punishment for the son's iniquity."*

In another Scripture passage the Lord makes a similar objection to the same generational curse proverb. In Jeremiah 31:29-34 we read: "In those days they shall say no more: 'The fathers have eaten sour grapes, and the children's teeth are set on edge.' But every one shall die for his own iniquity; every man who eats the sour grapes, his teeth shall be set on edge."

Thus, we see in the Bible God is objecting to the concept of generational curse by the messages of two prophets. Isn't that adequate indication of God's affirmed objection to the erroneous concept of generational curse?

In both Scripture passages in Ezekiel and Jeremiah the Lord forthrightly objected to the generational curse proverb that "the fathers eat the sour grapes, but the children's teeth are set on edge" and forbade the children of Israel from using it. Then He categorically stated His justice in dealing with sinners. *According to His justice, God will not punish the innocent descendants for the sins of guilty ancestors.* The guilty individual will bear his own punishment.

God's Design

> ❖ *God's people are a people of purpose and destiny designed by God. Their lives' events are not controlled or determined by the evil omens of sorcerers.*

The Bible makes it plain that *"all things* work together for good to those who love God, to those who are the called according to His purpose" (Romans 8:28). All things include both pleasant and unpleasant experiences. God's people are a people of purpose and destiny designed by God. Their lives' events are not controlled or determined by the evil omens of sorcerers. "The steps of a good man are ordered by the Lord, and He delights in his way" (Psalm 37:23).

As we mentioned already, the erroneous conception of God's blessings as synonymous to material prosperity and ease blinds people to the goodness of God's design in even the adverse things that come their way.

The story of Job is a revelation to God's people that God has a divine hedge of protection around us and Satan himself, who goes to and fro in the earth with the aim to devour and destroy God's people, respects this hedge which he cannot penetrate without God's permission. Therefore, when Job was bitterly tried he refused to acknowledge it was the work of Satan or some sort of evil omen. Instead, in the midst of his adversities Job maintained His confidence in the supreme control and design of God over his life.

Job accepted God's design in all that was happening to him. He kept his worship of God without murmuring or charging God wrongfully. We read in Job 1:20-22: "Then Job arose, tore his robe, and shaved his head; and he fell to the ground and worshiped. And he said: 'Naked I came from my mother's womb, and naked shall I return there. *The Lord gave, and the Lord has taken away; blessed be the name of the Lord.*' In all this, Job did not sin nor charge God with wrong."

God may allow adversities in the lives of His people, but these adversities are not curses but blessings in disguise. God allows trials in our lives when they are necessary and beneficial to us and are meant to bring glory to Him and to confound Satan, the adversary of God and of our souls. We who believe in Christ must not despise adversities, but when we are being tried we should commit ourselves to God with the assurance that the adversities we go through in no way mean God is against us or has left us to the scourge of some curse unleashed on us by men or devils. Let us stand on the promises of the Holy Scriptures and not on myths so that we may find genuine comfort and peace from God in times of adversities.

We read in Romans 8:35-37: "Who shall separate us from the love of Christ? Shall tribulation, or distress, or persecution, or famine, or nakedness, or peril, or sword? As it is written, 'For Your sake we are killed all the day long. We are counted as sheep of slaughter.' But in all these things we more than conquer through Him who loved us."

First Corinthians 10:13 reminds us: "No temptation has overtaken you except such as is common to man; but God is faithful, who will not allow you to be tempted beyond what you are able, but with the temptation will also make the way of escape, that you may be able to bear it."

Further insight into God's design for our trials is given to us in 1 Peter 1:6-7: "In this you greatly rejoice, though now for a little while, if need be, you have been grieved by various trials, that the genuineness of your faith, being much more precious than gold that perishes, though it is tested by fire, may be found to praise, honour, and glory at the revelation of Jesus Christ."

No Scriptural Basis

Therefore we see that the misleading doctrine of the generational curse has no basis in the Scriptures. It has no foundation in the Old Testament and in the New Testament. It is an affront to God's character of mercy and divine justice and is denounced by God. Therefore the generational curse doctrine is unscriptural.

God is merciful and gracious. Far from punishing innocent descendants for the sins of guilty ancestors, the Lord forgives and justifies all sinners who repent and put their faith in Jesus Christ. Therefore, under the New Covenant of grace even the curse of sin inherited by the entire human race is removed in Christ Jesus.

To believe or propagate the generational curse falsehood is to deny God's faithfulness and justice in keeping His covenant. Believers in Christ must be constantly on guard against the wiles of Satan to deceive them into distrusting the faithfulness of God. Having no basis at all in the Scriptures and plainly denounced by God in the Scriptures, the generational curse doctrine is a myth from the pit of hell.

The truth of the Word of God in uncovering the generational curse myth is being presented plainly in this book. The Word of the Lord is truth that makes us free and generates faith in the hearts of all who truly believe. "So then faith comes by hearing, and hearing by the word of God" (Romans 10:17).

The generational curse myth, on the contrary, brings those who adhere to it into bondage of fear and unbelief. People who believe the generational curse myth is truth usually are relentlessly tormented with fear. They interpret every adversity in their lives as evidence of a curse. They are blinded to the comforting truth that the goodness of God, and not evil, is in everything God allows in His people's lives.

Liberation from the Idea

> ❖ *The way out of the bondage of fear imposed by the generational curse myth is simply to renounce the myth and accept the liberating truth of the Word of God.*

The truth is that, in the light of the Scriptures, God has neither pronounced nor sanctioned any generational curse. The Scriptures clearly state that God categorically forbids the upholding of such an unjust concept.

How can one be liberated then from the perceived misery of being under a generational curse? Jesus declares in John 8:32: "And you shall know the truth, and the truth shall make you free."

The way out of the bondage of fear imposed by the generational curse myth is simply to renounce the myth and accept the liberating truth of the Word of God. Truth dispels the illusion of lies and liberates the mind from the bondage of darkness. Anyone who has been a victim of the fearful illusion of being under a generational curse can find full deliverance by the faith-inspiring and enlightening scriptural truths presented in this book.

7. Removal of the Curse of Sin

Removal of the Curse of Sin through Christ

> ❖ *The fact that in Christ the curse of sin is removed means that no believer in Christ, of whatever family lineage, can be affected by any curse, including a so-called generational curse.*

We mentioned at the beginning of this study that every human being born on earth from generation to generation inherits the curse of sin from Adam. The Bible tells us in Romans 5:12: "Through one man sin entered the world, and death through sin, and thus death spread to all men, because all sinned."

So in that sense every one of us, in spite of individual genealogy or ancestors, race or culture, was born under the curse of sin because of our descent from Adam. As we noted, however, this is unlike the generational curse myth, which holds that generational curses are curses transmitted through particular family lineages.

Nevertheless, any sin committed by a man, in whatever family or tribe, is a consequence of the fall of man. Those who propagate the myth of the generational curse as a curse upon specific family lineages must explain why, if all have sinned, certain families must be punished with generational curses and not others. The concept of generational curses being inherited within particular family lineages has absolutely no place under the New Covenant of grace in which every believer in Christ stands in the righteousness of God and is pronounced justified or not guilty by God by grace. In other words, the fact that in Christ the curse of sin is removed means that no believer in Christ, of whatever family lineage, can be affected by any curse, including a so-called generational curse.

That declaration is made clearly in Romans 5:17-19: *"For if by the one man's offence death reined through the one, much more those who receive abundance of grace and of the gift of righteousness will rein in life through the One, Jesus Christ. Therefore, as through one man's offence judgment came to all men, resulting in condemnation, even so through one Man's righteous act the free gift came to all men, resulting in justification of life. For as by one man's disobedience many were made sinners, so also by one Man's obedience many will be made righteous."*

Law and Grace

Jeremiah, in direct reference to the false concept of a generational curse, proclaimed through prophecy the truth of the universal curse of sin being removed through Christ under the New Covenant of grace. Interestingly, Jeremiah links God's denunciation of the generational curse proverb with the prophetic announcement of God's introduction of the New Covenant of grace.

We read in Jeremiah 31:29-34: *"In those days they will not say again, 'the fathers have eaten sour grapes, and the children's teeth are set on edge.' But everyone will die for his own iniquity; each man who eats the sour grapes, his teeth will be set on edge. 'Behold, days are coming,' declares the Lord, 'when I will make a new covenant with the house of*

Israel and with the house of Judah, not like the covenant which I made with their fathers in the day I took them by the hand to bring them out of the land of Egypt, My covenant which they broke, although I was a husband to them,' declares the Lord. 'But this is the covenant which I will make with the house of Israel after those days,' declares the Lord; 'I will put My law within them and on their heart I will write it; and I will be their God, and they shall be My people. They will not teach again, each man his neighbour and each man his brother, saying, 'Know the Lord,' for they will all know Me, from the least of them to the greatest of them,' declares the Lord, 'for I will forgive their iniquity, and their sin I will remember no more.'"

Under the Old Covenant, sin and the curse of sin became defined by the Law of Moses. Sinful man, being unable to keep the Law, had to face inevitably the penalties prescribed for breaking the Law. The inherent inability of sinful man to keep the Law and the judgmental consequences of breaking the Law were considered to be the curse of the Law or the curse of sin. But under the New Covenant of grace God has brought to mankind deliverance from sin and the curse of the Law through the atoning work of Christ Jesus.

We read in Galatians 3:10-14: "For as many as are out of works of the Law, these are under a curse; for it is written, 'Cursed is everyone who does not continue in all things which are written in the Book of the Law, to do them.' But that no one is justified by the Law in the sight of God is clear, for, 'The just shall live by faith.' But the Law is not of faith; but, 'The man who does these things shall live in them.' Christ redeemed us from the curse of the Law, being made a curse for us (for it is written, 'Cursed is everyone having been hanged on a tree'); so that the blessing of Abraham might be to the nations in Jesus Christ, and that we might receive the promise of the Spirit through faith."

The curse of the Law is a curse which is a consequence of the sin which all men of every tribe and race have inherited and cannot be regarded as applied particularly to any one class of people, for example, a particular race or family. Christ, through His redemptive work on Calvary, has redeemed us from the dominion of sin and the curse of the Law and has bestowed upon us the eternal blessings of God.

Therefore, all of mankind are invited to embrace the redemptive work of Christ as their only means of deliverance from the universal curse of sin. All who come to believe in Christ, of whatever tribe, nation or family lineage, are no longer under any curse of sin but are blessed in Christ with all spiritual blessings by God.

8. The Generational Blessing

The New Covenant of Blessing

❖ *Instead of supporting the myth of a generational curse concept, the gospel heralds the good news of a true generational blessing to all nations and generations who through faith in Christ become offspring of Abraham's seed and inheritors of the universal Abrahamic covenant of blessing.*

Let us explore the concept of a generational blessing being a Scripture-based replacement for the unscriptural concept of a generational curse. Under the Law of Moses in the Old Covenant, Moses declared blessings upon all who kept the Law and curses upon all who disobeyed the Law (Deuteronomy 28). Therefore, since sin dominated human nature, and no one could keep the Law, the curse of the Law was upon the Jews and all mankind, according to the Old Covenant. "For as many as are out of works of the Law, these are under a curse;... 'Cursed is everyone who does not continue in all things which are written in the Book of the Law, to do them'" (Galatians 3:10). Thus the curse of the Law, as we mentioned before, became identified with the universal curse of sin.

The New Covenant gives man the opportunity to be liberated from the curse of the Law through the atoning work of Jesus Christ on the cross of Calvary. Hence, in Christ Jesus the people of all nations may be delivered from the curse of sin or the curse of the Law. This is the good news of the gospel. "Christ redeemed us from the curse of the Law, being made a curse for us (for it is written, 'Cursed is everyone having been hanged on a tree'); *so that the blessing of Abraham might be to the nations in Jesus Christ,* and that we might receive the promise of the Spirit through faith" (Galatians 3:13-14). Praise the Lord!

The Abrahamic Covenant of Blessing

Four hundred and thirty years before God established the nation of Israel through the Old Covenant and the Law of Moses, God established a covenant with Abraham that He would bless the nations through Abraham's Seed (Genesis 22:18). Abraham's Seed actually refers to Christ in whom all the nations of the earth are blessed through faith.

In fact, we must note that this universal covenant of blessing through the Seed goes back to God's promise after the fall of man in the Garden of Eden to bring redemption to mankind through the Seed of the woman. God had declared to the devil that had deceived man into disobedience to God in the Garden of Eden: "And I will put enmity between you and the woman, and between your seed and her *Seed*; He will bruise your head, and you shall bruise His heel" (Genesis 3:15).

Christ effectively fulfilled God's promise of redemption for mankind by defeating the devil and bringing deliverance to mankind from the devil's bondage, according to the Scriptures: "Since then the children have partaken of flesh and blood, He also Himself likewise partook of the same;

that through death He might destroy him who had the power of death (that is, the devil), and deliver those who through fear of death were all their lifetime subject to bondage" (Hebrews 2:14-15).

A Universal Covenant of Blessing

Under the Old Covenant the covenant of blessing was confined specifically to the nation of Israel on the condition that they kept the Law. As we have already noted, unable to keep the Law, the Jewish nation, with whom the Old Covenant was established, invariably came under the curse of the Law. Hence, both Jews and Gentiles, as descendants of Adam came under the universal curse of sin since all sinned.

But the curse of the Law could not annul the preceding covenant God made with Abraham to bless all nations in Christ through faith. Paul explains this in Galatians 3:16-18: "And to Abraham and to his Seed the promises were spoken. It does not say, 'And to seeds,' as of many; but as of one, 'And to your Seed,' which is Christ. And I say this, A covenant having been ratified by God in Christ, the Law (coming into being four hundred and thirty years after) does not annul the promise, so as to abolish it. For if the inheritance is of Law, it is no more of promise; but God gave it to Abraham by way of promise."

The Scriptures, therefore, make it clear that through the Abrahamic covenant every human being of every nation — Jew or Gentile — by believing in Christ becomes a beneficiary of the universal covenant of blessing God established with Abraham. And, furthermore, *the curse of no nation, family or individual can annul the universal Abrahamic covenant of blessing.*

The truth is, according to the Scriptures, that God established this universal covenant of blessing with Abraham on the basis of faith and not on the basis of race, genealogy or heredity. Thus, faith in Christ rather than hereditary connection to Abraham became the basis on which one is blessed with the blessing of Abraham.

Paul explains in Galatians 3:6-9: "Even as Abraham believed God, and it was counted to him for righteousness. Therefore *know that those of faith, these are the sons of Abraham*. And the Scripture, foreseeing that God would justify the nations through faith, preached the gospel before to Abraham, saying, *'In you shall all nations be blessed.' So then those of faith are blessed with faithful Abraham*."

It is interesting to note again at this point that even if one were to perceive the curse of sin through Adam or the curse of the Law through the Jews as support for a generational curse concept, the truth of the universal blessing of God upon all nations in Christ through the Abrahamic covenant cancels any concept or effect of such a hereditary curse.

As far as the curse of sin on the human race through Adam is concerned, the Scriptures tell us that Christ replaced Adam as the universal Head or Father of all who through faith in Christ become a new breed of creatures in Christ (2 Corinthians 5:17). We read in 1 Corinthians 15:21-22, 47-49: "For since death is through man, the resurrection of the dead also is through a Man. *For as in Adam all die, even so in Christ all will be made alive....* The first man was out of earth, earthy; the second Man was the Lord from Heaven. Such the earthy man, such also the earthy ones. And such the heavenly Man, such also the heavenly ones. And according as we bore the image of the earthy man, we shall also bear the image of the heavenly Man."

In a similar manner, as far as the curse of the Law through the Jews is concerned, Christ also has provided redemption from the curse of the Law. As we referred to before, "Christ redeemed us from the curse of the Law, being made a curse for us (for it is written, 'Cursed is everyone having been hanged on a tree'); so that the blessing of Abraham might be to the nations in Jesus Christ, and that we might receive the promise of the Spirit through faith" (Galatians 3:13-14).

Hence, *believers in Christ, far from being under a generational curse, are under the universal generational blessing of God in Christ, the last Adam.* Paul summarizes this wonderful truth of the universal generational blessing of God upon all nations in Christ this way in Galatians 3:22-28: "But the Scripture shut up all under sin, so that the promise by faith of Jesus Christ might be given to those who believe. But before faith came, we were kept under Law, having been shut up to the faith about to be revealed. So that the Law has become a trainer of us until Christ, that we might be justified by faith. But faith coming, we are no longer under a trainer. For you are all sons of God through faith in Christ Jesus. For as many as were baptized into Christ, you put on Christ. There cannot be Jew or Greek, there is neither bond nor free, there is neither male nor female; for you are all one in Christ Jesus. And if you are Christ's, then you are Abraham's seed and heirs according to the promise."

The Generational Blessing Gospel

Hence, instead of supporting the myth of a generational curse concept, the gospel heralds the good news of a true generational blessing to all nations and generations who through faith in Christ become offspring of Abraham's seed, the last Adam, and inheritors of the universal Abrahamic covenant of blessing. People of all nations, tribes and families can now experience the blessedness of God in Christ. Peter declares to all believers in Christ in 1 Peter 2:9-10: "But you are a chosen generation, a royal priesthood, a holy nation, His own special people, that you may proclaim the praises of Him who called you out of darkness into His marvellous light; who once were not a people but are now the people of God, who had not obtained mercy but now have obtained mercy."

Let us embrace the truth of the gospel, the good news of the generational blessings of God upon all believers in Christ. The myth of the generational curse doctrine brings bondage and fear, making it evident that it is not from God. Fear brings torment, and that is what the myth of the generational curse doctrine has generated in the minds of those who have become ensnared by it. The truth of the Word of God, however, does not generate fear and bondage in the minds and lives of His people. "For you did not receive the spirit of bondage again to fear, but you received the Spirit of adoption by whom we cry out, 'Abba, Father'. For God has not given us a spirit of fear, but of power and of love and of a sound mind" (Romans 8:15; 2 Timothy 1:7).

9. The Genealogy of Jesus Christ

Rahab and Ruth

❖ *It is interesting to note that in the book of the genealogy of Jesus Christ the Scriptures do not conceal the names of Rahab and Ruth as ancestors of Jesus Christ.*

The propagators of the myth of the generational curse usually search the genealogical history of families to identify ancestors of disrepute as sources of the generational curses they claim to be upon the descendant families. Some even strongly advise against marriage into families whom they claim to have ancestors who are of disrepute and thus may be sources of generational curses. But it is interesting to note that in the book of the genealogy of Jesus Christ the Scriptures do not conceal the names of Rahab and Ruth as ancestors of Jesus Christ (Matthew 1:5).

Who was Rahab and who was Ruth that they should be particularly mentioned by their names among the very few women listed in the book of the genealogy of Jesus Christ in the Bible? Ironically, neither Rahab nor Ruth may be considered among women of reputable virtue.

Rahab was a harlot, an occupation of disrepute in ancient times as it is today (Joshua 2:1-22; 6:22-25; Hebrews 11:31; James 2:25). Nonetheless, she gave shelter and protection to the two Hebrew spies who were sent by Joshua to scout Jericho when the Israelites were about to enter Canaan (Joshua 2:1-24). Justified and blessed by God through faith, she became the mother of Boaz, who married Ruth, a Moabite woman, who gave birth to Obed, who was the father of Jesse, the father of King David. She is particularly mentioned by name in the Scriptures in the genealogy of Jesus Christ (Matthew 1:5-6).

Ruth was of the tribe of the Moabites, descendants of Moab, who was born from an incestuous relationship between Lot and his daughter (Genesis 19:36-37). God once forbade the children of Israel to have any association with the Moabites. We read in Deuteronomy 23:3-26: "An Ammonite or Moabite shall not enter the assembly of the Lord; even to the tenth generation none of his descendants shall enter the assembly of the Lord forever, because they did not meet you with bread and water on the road when you came out of Egypt, and because they hired against you Balaam the son of Beor from Pethor of Mesopotamia, to curse you. Nevertheless the Lord your God would not listen to Balaam, but the Lord your God turned the curse into a blessing for you, because the Lord your God loves you. You shall not seek their peace or their prosperity all your days forever." Yet Ruth, though a Moabite descendant, became an ancestor of Jesus Christ and is particularly mentioned in the genealogical generation of Jesus Christ.

Rahab and Ruth were not Hebrews and were clearly of disreputable generations, but when by faith they accepted the God of the Hebrews they became participators in the generational blessing of Abraham and were chosen to be among the ancestors of Jesus Christ. The selection of Rahab and Ruth by God to be in the lineage of the ancestors of Jesus Christ, the Son of God, demonstrates that the myth of the generational curse has absolutely no divine foundation.

The Genealogy of a Christian

❖ *The genealogy of a Christian originates in Christ and not from human ancestors.*

The myth of the generational curse is based on natural or human genealogy. It assumes that because of human genealogy by which one inherits physical traits from one's ancestors, one also may inherit spiritual traits. Hence, it is assumed that one can inherit a curse through genealogical transmission of that curse from generation to generation.

A curse is a spiritual omen. We know that spiritual traits, unlike physical traits, cannot be genetically transmitted. But, even if one were to accept the erroneous assumption of the generational transmission of a curse, the truth of the new birth every believer in Christ enters into destroys the argument that Christians can be under a generational curse. In the realm of the kingdom of God the new birth of believers in Christ implies an end to their former human genealogical connections.

The genealogy of a Christian originates in Christ and not from human ancestors. John describes the birth and origin of a Christian in this way: "But as many as received Him, He gave to them authority to become the children of God, to those who believe on His name, *who were born, not of blood, nor of the will of the flesh, nor of the will of man, but were born of God*" (John 1:12-13).

The Christian life does not have its origin or source in humanity. The Christian life has its birth in God. Every believer in Christ is a new creature who is no longer connected to the first Adam and his fallen nature but is spiritually connected to the last Adam, Jesus Christ. Christians are no longer inheritors of the corrupt nature and heritage of the first Adam but are now joint heirs with Christ of the fullness of the blessings of God.

Paul, the apostle, expounds this deep and glorious truth to us in this manner in 1 Corinthians 15:44-49: "There is a natural body, and there is a spiritual body. And so it is written, 'The first man Adam became a living being.' The last Adam became a life giving spirit. However, the spiritual is not first, but the natural, and afterward the spiritual. *The first man was of the earth, made of dust; the second Man is the Lord from heaven. As was the man of dust, so also are those who are made of dust; and as is the heavenly Man, so also are those who are heavenly. And as we have borne the image of the man of dust, we shall also bear the image of the heavenly Man.*"

Hence, one who accepts the truth of the new birth of a Christian cannot uphold the idea that, if curses were transmissible by genealogical connections, a Christian can rightly inherit any curse from his natural ancestors. By being born again of God, the believer in Christ becomes an offspring of God. Let us explore further the truth of the born-again nature of a Christian.

Know Who You Are in Christ

> ❖ *Believers in Christ possess supernatural attributes which equip them as sons of God to be constant conquerors over the adversities and attacks of Satan.*

The profound truth is that a believer in Christ is a partaker of divine nature by which he is freed from worldly corruption. This astounding truth is declared by Peter in 2 Peter 1:3-4: "His divine power has given to us all things that pertain to life and godliness, through the knowledge of Him who called us by glory and virtue, by which have been given to us exceedingly great and precious promises, that through these you may be partakers of the divine nature, having escaped the corruption that is in the world through lust."

Far from being miserably and inevitably subjected to superstitious curses, as the propagators of the myth of the generational curse would want us to believe, believers in Christ are made to partake of the divine nature by which they are liberated from the corruption of this world. They derive supernatural attributes from the divine nature and are spiritually equipped to be constant conquerors over the adversities and attacks of Satan.

Paul writes: "What then shall we say to these things? If God is for us, who can be against us? Truly He who did not spare His own Son, but delivered Him up for us all, how shall He not with Him also freely give us all things? Who shall lay anything to the charge of God's elect? It is God who justifies. Who is he condemning? It is Christ who has died, but rather also who is raised, who is also at the right hand of God, who also intercedes for us. Who shall separate us from the love of Christ? Shall tribulation, or distress, or persecution, or famine, or nakedness, or peril, or sword? As it is written, 'For Your sake we are killed all the day long. We are counted as sheep of slaughter.' But in all these things we more than conquer through Him who loved us" (Romans 8:31-37).

God's Own Special People

Christians, indeed, are God's own special people. They appear to be natural, but they are not merely natural human beings. They are virtually a supernatural people. This is God's doing, and no one should despise it or underestimate it. According to Paul, it is "the great God and our Saviour Jesus Christ; who gave Himself for us, that He might redeem us from every lawless deed and purify for Himself *His own special people*, zealous for good works" (Titus 2:13-14).

Peter too makes a similar declaration in 1 Peter 2:9-10: "But you are a chosen generation, a royal priesthood, a holy nation, *His own special people*, that you may proclaim the praises of Him who called you out of darkness into His marvellous light; who once were not a people but are now the people of God, who had not obtained mercy but now have obtained mercy."

The second birth distinguishes Christians from the rest of the human race. Through the second birth, as we have already discussed, God is reproducing a new breed of people. Christians represent the second Adamic race which God is bringing forth in the life and attributes and character of Christ, the Son of God. Every true Christian has the very life of Christ within and, like Paul, the apostle, can declare confidently and triumphantly, "I have been crucified with Christ; it is no longer I who live, but Christ lives in me" (Galatians 2:20).

According to the Scriptures, the truth of Christ in us is the mystery hidden in ages past but now made clear by the Holy Spirit in this age of grace. It is "the mystery which has been hidden from ages and from generations, but now has been revealed to His saints. To them God willed to make known what are the riches of the glory of this mystery among the Gentiles: which is *Christ in you*, the hope of glory" (Colossians 1:26-27).

It is the presence of the Christ in our frail human body that makes us mysteriously invincible to the trials and tribulations which confront us in this world. In this way our extraordinary resilience and triumph in the midst of adversities glorify God since they demonstrate that the ability with which we operate is certainly not of our humanity but of God.

Paul puts it this way: "But we have this treasure in earthen vessels that the excellence of the power may be of God and not of us. We are hard-pressed on every side, yet not crushed; we are perplexed, but not in despair; persecuted, but not forsaken; struck down, but not destroyed—always carrying about in the body the dying of the Lord Jesus, that the life of Jesus also may be manifested in our body" (2 Corinthians 4:7-10).

Sons of God

> ❖ *If Christians will know who they are by believing and accepting what the Word of God declares they are in Christ, then they can in no way accept the myth that they are subjected to generational curses.*

In fact, a wonderful truth Christians need to be made aware of is that God has put the Spirit of His Son into believers in Christ to adopt them as sons of God. Yes, indeed! We are sons of God in the midst of this world!

Yet there are those who will have us underestimate who we are and perceive ourselves to be subjected to the vain superstitious traditions and elements of the lower realms of this world. Paul puts it well this way in Galatians 4:6-10: "And because you are sons, God has sent forth the Spirit of His Son into your hearts, crying out, 'Abba, Father!' Therefore you are no longer a slave but a son, and if a son, then an heir of God through Christ. *But then, indeed, when you did not know God, you served those which by nature are not gods. But now after you have known God, or rather are known by God, how is it that you turn again to the weak and beggarly elements, to which you desire again to be in bondage? You observe days and months and seasons and years.*"

Many Christians need to rise up to their full God-given Christian potential. They also need to know who they are. It is their lack of awareness of who they really are that makes it possible for false teaching like the myth of the generational curse to be accepted and even propagated by so many Christians. Therefore, if Christians know who they are by believing and accepting what the Word of God declares they are in Christ, then they can in no way accept the myth that they are subjected to generational curses.

10. Blessed in Christ

The Good News

> ❖ *"Blessed be the God and Father of our Lord Jesus Christ, who has blessed us with every spiritual blessing in heavenly places in Christ."*

In light of all that we have discussed so far from the Scriptures, the good news of the gospel is that every believer in Christ is blessed. Let us now explore the dimensions of this blessedness which every believer has in Christ Jesus.

We read in Ephesians 1:3: "Blessed be the God and Father of our Lord Jesus Christ, who has blessed us with every spiritual blessing in heavenly places in Christ."

This Scripture passage plainly asserts that there is no curse whatsoever hanging upon the believer in Christ. No one can curse whom God has blessed. God has thoroughly blessed every believer in Christ. It is not a promise but an accomplished fact. Being thoroughly blessed of God is synonymous to being a Christian—being in Christ. Therefore these blessings are not bestowed upon believers through their prayer and supplication or by anyone's prayer on their behalf. These blessings are provided already by God in Christ for every believer who abides in Christ.

Those who propagate the generational curse myth usually assume for themselves the presumptuous role of dispelling the so-called generational curse and bestowing the blessings of God upon believers in Christ. This is indeed arrogance on the part of mortal man to assume a curse where God has not put a curse, and to proceed to break the assumed curse when God has already broken all curse freely by His own will and grace through Christ.

God is faithful, and what He declares He has done, He has done. God keeps His covenant. The New Covenant by which all believers are entitled to be thoroughly blessed in Christ has been sealed by the blood of Jesus Christ, the Son of God. No one can add or take away from the benefits prescribed in the New Covenant or improve on the redeeming work of Christ. *And if all the hosts of hell were to assail to challenge the surety of God's covenant of blessings, they shall be effectively defeated by the Christ Himself, who is the mediator of the New Covenant.* Therefore, believers in Christ are invariably blessed by God with all spiritual blessings in the heavenly realm, and no one can add or take away from the blessings God has faithfully bestowed on believers through Christ.

Accomplished, Comprehensive, Spiritual, Heavenly and in Christ

> ❖ *The blessedness of a believer in Christ is accomplished, comprehensive, spiritual, heavenly and in Christ.*

The blessings God has bestowed upon believers in Christ have five principal characteristics we will examine in this section. These five principal characteristics of the blessings of God upon a believer indicate the comprehensiveness and sufficiency of these blessings in all aspects of a believer's life, as well as the invincibility of these blessings against all sorts of natural and diabolical forces.

The blessedness of a believer in Christ is characterized as being *accomplished, comprehensive, spiritual, heavenly and in Christ*. These five characteristics of our blessedness in Christ are depicted in Ephesians 1:3: "Blessed be the God and Father of our Lord Jesus Christ, *who has blessed* us with *all spiritual blessings in heavenly places in Christ*." Let us explore these five wonderful dimensions of the blessedness of a believer in Christ.

Accomplished

First, the Scripture passage in Ephesians 1:3 asserts plainly that God *has blessed* the believer in Christ. This means that the bestowal of the blessings of God upon a believer in Christ is *accomplished*. It is an accomplished fact. It has been performed fully by God. God has blessed us who believe in Christ. Hence, we are completely blessed by God.

The comforting truth that our blessedness in Christ is an accomplished fact is brought out in Balaam's statement concerning the irreversibility of God's blessing upon the nation of Israel in Numbers 23:19-20: "God is not a man, that He should lie, nor a son of man, that He should repent. Has He said, and will He not do it? Or has He spoken, and will He not make it good? Behold, I have received a command to bless; *He has blessed, and I cannot reverse it*."

Balaam discovered this wonderful truth when he was hired by King Balak to curse the people of Israel in the wilderness of Sinai. He quickly recognized that God had already blessed Israel. He had to admit to Balak that God who had blessed Israel was faithful and unchangeable. In other words, when God has blessed, no one can reverse it. It is an accomplished fact, and no one can change it.

Comprehensive

Second, these blessings represent *all* spiritual blessings in the heavenly realms. The blessings God has bestowed on believers in Christ are *comprehensive*. They lack nothing and constitute every blessing there is. The word "all" is self-explicit and essentially means there is nothing left out in a specified category. The Holy Spirit does not use words in vain. Therefore, when the Holy Spirit declares in the Holy Scriptures that the all-knowing and all-resourceful God has bestowed *all* blessings, the comprehensiveness of these blessings is obvious, as well as indisputable. No blessing is left out.

Peter describes the comprehensiveness of God's blessings upon us who believe in Christ in this way in 2 Peter 1:2-4: "Grace and peace be multiplied to you in the knowledge of God and of Jesus our Lord, as *His divine power has given to us all things that pertain to life and godliness,* through the knowledge of Him who called us by glory and virtue, by which have been given to us exceedingly great and precious promises, that through these you may be partakers of the divine nature, having escaped the corruption that is in the world through lust."

Paul also depicts this truth vividly in 2 Corinthians 9:8: "God is able to make *all grace abound* toward you, that you, *always having all sufficiency in all things,* may have *abundance for every good work.*" Note the use of the comprehensive word "all" in the Scripture passage.

Spiritual

Third, these blessings are *spiritual blessings*. This implies that these blessings do not originate from the natural realm. They are neither connected to, nor dependent on, the natural.

Being spiritual, these blessings transcend the transient assets of the flesh or human resources. Hence, human genealogy, race, tribe, family or bloodline has absolutely nothing to do with these blessings. According to Jesus, what originates from the flesh is flesh, and what originates from the Spirit is spirit (John 3:3).

Natural environment and human and natural resources may be means by which these blessings are experienced, but they are not determinants of the spiritual blessings of God. These blessings are of the Spirit and are bestowed and sustained by the Spirit of God. To be blessed spiritually is to be blessed in a manner that nothing natural can affect. Where natural means are necessary to transmit these spiritual blessings, God will use natural means. If a natural means fail, another will be used. If no natural means seem to be available, God can by-pass or create natural means, but nothing can annul God's spiritual blessings where He has commanded them.

Heavenly

Fourth, these blessings are *heavenly blessings*. They are rooted in the heavenly realm. They originate in the heavens. This has significant implication in terms of the authority and power of the heavenly over the earthly.

The psalmist David marvellously unfolds the truth of the superiority of the heavenly over all that which is of the earth, including man and the natural environment, in Psalm 103:13-19: "As a father pities his children, so the Lord pities those who fear Him. For He knows our frame; He remembers that we are dust. As for man, his days are like grass; as a flower of the field, so he flourishes. For the wind passes over it, and it is gone, and its place remembers it no more. But the mercy of the Lord is from everlasting to everlasting on those who fear Him, and His righteousness to children's children, to such as keep His covenant, and to those who remember

His commandments to do them. *The Lord has established His throne in heaven, and His kingdom rules over all."*

Nebuchadnezzar, king of Babylon, who because of his arrogance was dramatically and tragically judged by God, was informed when the judgment was pronounced on him, "your kingdom shall be assured to you, after you come to know that *heaven rules*" (Daniel 4:26). "Then he was driven from the sons of men, his heart was made like the beasts, and his dwelling was with the wild donkeys. They fed him with grass like oxen, and his body was wet with the dew of heaven, *till he knew that the Most High God rules in the kingdom of men, and appoints over it whomever He chooses*" (Daniel 5:21).

Our Lord Jesus advises us of the far greater security of the things of heaven than the things of earth in this way: "Do not lay up for yourselves treasures on earth, where moth and rust destroy and where thieves break in and steal; but lay up for yourselves treasures in heaven, where neither moth nor rust destroys and where thieves do not break in and steal" (Matthew 6:19-20).

Therefore, to be blessed with "blessings in heavenly places" is to be blessed with blessings which are superior to all the earth has to offer. It also means to be blessed by a divine authority that cannot be withstood by anyone or anything on earth. Finally, it means to be blessed with blessings which are sure, secure and incorruptible unlike the corruptible things of the earth, even such like silver and gold.

In Christ

Fifth and final, but certainly not the least, these blessings are rooted *in Christ*. What does that imply? It implies that the blessings of God upon a believer in Christ are attributable solely to Christ. These blessings have absolutely nothing to do with our human status, ability, genealogy or environment.

These blessings have nothing to do with us. These blessings are in Christ and Christ alone. Hence, believers in Christ are blessed because they are in Christ. Anyone who is in Christ is invariably blessed thoroughly with God's blessings that are in Christ.

Every Christian is essentially in Christ. According to the Scriptures, one becomes a Christian by being baptized or immersed and absorbed into Christ: "For as many *of you as were baptized into Christ* have put on Christ" (Galatians 3:27). In other words, the Christian character is derived from Christ. One cannot be a Christian without being in Christ.

A Christian is a new creation in Christ. Virtually all spiritual connection to the old Adamic nature and human genealogy is severed in Christ: "Therefore, if anyone is *in Christ,* he is a new creation; old things have passed away; behold: all things have become new" (2 Corinthians 5:17).

One can live a genuine Christian life only by abiding in Christ: "*Abide in Me,* and I in you. As the branch cannot bear fruit of itself, unless it abides in the vine, neither can you, unless you abide in Me" (John 15:4).

A believer in Christ lacks nothing but is made complete or perfect in Christ. "For in Him dwells all the fullness of the Godhead bodily; and *you are complete in Him,* who is the head of all principality and power" (Colossians 2:9-10).

One more wonderful characteristic of being in Christ is that a believer in Christ is inseparable from the love of God. "For I am persuaded that neither death nor life, nor angels nor principalities nor powers, nor things present nor things to come, nor height nor depth, nor any other created thing, shall be able to separate us from the love of God which is *in Christ Jesus our Lord*" (Romans 8:38-39).

The point in all of these wonderful Scripture passages is that a genuine Christian is one who is invariably in Christ, and hence, if in Christ, is invariably blessed by God with all spiritual blessings in heavenly places in Christ. Then who, whether ancestors, sorcery or evildoers, can deprive or hinder a believer in Christ from being blessed? God has blessed the believer in Christ, and none can reverse it.

The Gospel

> ❖ *Ministers of God are not called to propagate fables and myths or to generate fear among believers through misleading teachings which have no foundation in the Word of God.*

The blessedness of all believers in Christ is the true gospel—the good news which God's ministers are sent to proclaim to all nations. Ministers of God are not called to propagate fables and myths or to generate fear among believers through misleading teachings which have no foundation in the Word of God. The myth of the generational curse seeks to rob believers of their peace and faith in the blessedness of the full salvation of God in Christ. God has given His servants a gospel of salvation, hope and blessings for mankind in the finished work of Christ on the cross.

Paul declares that the message which God has given His ministers to proclaim is a message of reconciliation between God and man. It is to announce the end of enmity between God and sinful man and the establishment of peace and goodwill from God towards man. We read in 2 Corinthians 5:18-21: "And all things are of God, who has reconciled us to Himself through Jesus Christ, and has given to us the ministry of reconciliation; whereas God was in Christ reconciling the world to Himself, not imputing their trespasses to them, and putting the word of reconciliation in us. Then we are ambassadors on behalf of Christ, as God exhorting through us, we beseech you on behalf of Christ, be reconciled to God. For He has made Him who knew no sin, to be sin for us, that we might become the righteousness of God in Him." This message is indeed contrary to a message of curse, as propagated by the generational curse myth.

We who are called to be ministers of God are authorized of God to proclaim the good news of the gospel—to declare to all men that Christ has come and has reconciled man to God. We are made ministers of this message of reconciliation, which speaks of life and peace and blessings for believers in fellowship and communion with God. With divine authority we must proclaim that everyone who believes in Christ is now reconciled to God or is at peace with God and is no longer under the wrath of God or the curse of sin, or any curse whatsoever.

Believers in Christ are justified or declared not guilty of their sins because Christ became the atonement for the sins of mankind. Therefore, there is no form of punishment which may be unleashed upon believers in Christ for their sins or the sins of their ancestors. Thus, no believer in Christ is under condemnation of any form. "There is therefore now *no condemnation to those who are in Christ Jesus,* who do not walk according to the flesh, but according to the Spirit" (Romans 8:1).

This is the good news of the gospel which ministers are ordained of God to proclaim. *Therefore we must be careful not to lend our support to the devil in despising the efficacious work of the atonement by Christ and declaring curses when God has pronounced blessings on all who believe in Christ.*

The truth of the blessings of God upon all believers in Christ is grounded in the New Covenant of grace introduced in Christ to mankind. By the New Covenant of grace God frees all who believe in Christ from guilt and condemnation. To deny this truth is to despise God's faithfulness in administering His promises in the New Covenant of grace. It is an affront to Christ and His redemptive work on the cross to mislead people into believing they are under generational curses, even after they have come to believe in Christ, rather than declaring to them the truth of their redemption by Christ from the curse of sin, including all the curses pronounced by the Law upon those who transgress the Law.

In highlighting the thorough effectiveness of the atoning work of Christ under the New Covenant, the Scriptures declare in Hebrews 9:13-15: "For if the blood of bulls and goats and the ashes of a heifer, sprinkling the unclean, sanctifies for the purifying of the flesh, how much more shall the blood of Christ, who through the eternal Spirit offered Himself without spot to God, cleanse your conscience from dead works to serve the living God? And for this reason He is the mediator of the new covenant, by means of death, for the redemption of the transgressions under the first covenant, that those who are called may receive the promise of the eternal inheritance."

11. Dip Your Buckets Where You Are

Blinding Myth

* *Superstitions and myths blind people to truth and reality.*

The myth of the generational curse doctrine seeks to blind believers to the glorious truth that God has blessed them in Christ and nothing can reverse the fact that their lives in Christ are thoroughly blessed. To accept the generational curse myth is to fail to recognize God's faithfulness and supreme power. It is to believe instead the lies of the devil that one's ancestors or some sort of sorcery can prevent God from bestowing upon a believer in Christ the blessings the Scriptures declare He has bestowed upon all believers in Christ.

Superstitions and myths blind people to truth and reality and seek to keep them in the torments of fear and darkness. That is exactly what the myth of the generational curse does to those who adhere to it. Therefore it is obvious why people who have accepted the myth of the generational curse appear to need deliverance. But the deliverance such people actually need is not from any so-called generational curse, which is just an illusion. Such people need deliverance from the torments of the fear and darkness generated by accepting the myth of the generational curse.

To obtain deliverance from the torments of the fear and darkness resulting from being deceived into accepting the myth of the generational curse doctrine, one obviously would have to become enlightened by the truth of the Word of God. Plainly, the Word of God declares that God has abundantly blessed all who believe in Christ. The truth of the Word of God liberates us from blindness, fear and deceit. This book employs the Word of God to plainly expose the myth and falsehood of the generational curse doctrine and to declare the truth of God's promised blessings upon us who believe in Christ. The light of this truth will completely dispel the darkness and fear produced by the illusion of generational curses in the minds of those who have been deceived by the myth.

An Unlimited Source

> ❖ *"I have come that they may have life, and that they may have it more abundantly."*

The promises of God's abundant provision laid down in the Bible for us are "exceedingly great and precious," and we must seek to know and embrace them by the grace of God and the revelation of the Spirit, who guides us into all truth. When we know the truth of the Word of God, we are made free from the blindness imposed by myths and lies of false religious doctrines. For instance, Jesus declares: "The thief does not come except to steal, and to kill, and to destroy. I have come that they may have life, and that they may have *it* more abundantly" (John 10:10). The abundance of the life given to believers in Christ supersedes all destructive works of evil.

The Myth of the Generational Curse

The story is told of a steam-engine ship that shut down and began to drift on the Atlantic Ocean. It sent out S.O.S. signals which were eventually picked up by another ship in the area. The ship signalled back that it was heading toward the distressed ship. Nightfall had come, and the distressed ship discovered it had also run out of fresh water and needed a supply. It sent out another S.O.S. signal requesting urgently a supply of fresh water. The ship signalled back to the distressed ship: "Dip your buckets where you are." Thinking the ship had misunderstood it needed fresh water, the distressed ship signalled again, "We need urgently fresh water." The ship signalled back, "Dip your buckets where you are." The distressed ship, knowing it was drifting on the Atlantic Ocean, signalled again its need for fresh water only to receive back the same response: "Dip your buckets where you are."

Eventually the captain of the distressed ship decided to follow the instructions and ordered that buckets be let down. The buckets were let down for water and lifted up. When the water was tasted it was found to be fresh water! Unknown to the captain on the distressed ship whose navigating instruments had shut down, his ship had drifted by nightfall into the estuary of one of the large rivers along the Atlantic Coast. There it was drifting on an infinite source of the fresh water it was in dire need of and yet begging for because it did not know.

Believers in Christ who might have become blinded by the myth of the generational curse are seeking desperately for blessings and deliverance from these assumed curses. Actually all they need is the revelation of the truth that already they are fully blessed in Christ and must simply dip their buckets where they are. Boldly dip into the vast unlimited source of blessings God has given you in Christ. Assert on the authority of the Word of God and the faithfulness of God that you are blessed, and do not give place to any lying thought or notion that you are under any curse. Accept the truth that you, who believe in Christ and have accepted God's salvation in Christ, are blessed with all spiritual blessings. The truth shall set you free from the bondage of fear generated by the myth of the ancestral curse doctrine.

Paul's prayer for the saints at Ephesus is so relevant to the needs of Christians misguided by the generational curse myth. "Therefore I...do not cease to give thanks for you, making mention of you in my prayers: that the God of our Lord Jesus Christ, the Father of glory, may give to you the spirit of wisdom and revelation in the knowledge of Him, the eyes of your understanding being enlightened; that you may know what is the hope of His calling, what are the riches of the glory of His inheritance in the saints, and what is the exceeding greatness of His power toward us who believe, according to the working of His mighty power which He worked in Christ when He raised Him from the dead and seated Him at His right hand in the heavenly places, far above all principality and power and might and dominion, and every name that is named, not only in this age but also in that which is to come. And He put all things under His feet, and gave Him to be head over all things to the church, which is His body, the fullness of Him who fills all in all" (Ephesians 1:15-23).

12. The Generational Curse Doctrine Is a Myth

Conclusion

❖ *The idea of a generational curse by which one is punished for the sins of ancestors is categorically opposed and rejected in the Scriptures.*

It is clear that the generational curse doctrine is a fear-generating myth derived from occultism and not from biblical truth. There is no generational curse. The idea of a generational curse is an illusion. Moreover, the concept of a generational curse by which one is punished for the sins of ancestors is categorically opposed and rejected in the Scriptures.

The Bible talks about the curse of the Law, or the universal curse of sin, which came upon the entire human race as a result of the fall. It is not the curse being referred to in the myth of the generational curse doctrine which, contrary to Scriptures, claims that a generational curse is a curse specific to certain family lineages and is therefore held to be distinct from the universal curse of sin.

As far as the universal curse of sin is concerned, the Scriptures present the good news that "Christ has redeemed us from the curse of the Law" in order that all nations might be blessed with the Abrahamic covenant blessings in Christ. Therefore, there is no curse or condemnation upon them who believe in Christ. All who believe in Christ are completely blessed by God in Christ.

As myths generally are, the generational curse doctrine has been accepted and propagated by those who adhere to it without proper investigation of its truthfulness in light of the Bible. Therefore, every believer in Christ must beware of this myth.

The Fundamental Truth of Christianity

❖ *If Christianity fundamentally rests upon belief in the atoning work of Christ on the cross, let us believe in it and gratefully accept its full benefits for all who are true Christian believers.*

Don't be beguiled by any preacher who claims you are under some sort of generational curse and that he is able to deliver you from such a curse. Such a curse does not exist. The idea of a generational curse is a myth. It has no foundation in the doctrines of the Bible.

All believers in Christ are truly blessed. Let no one deny you of your blessedness in Christ. Assert your blessedness in Christ on the authority of the Word of God and renounce the lies of Satan and his agents which try to trouble you with the myth of being cursed through your ancestors.

It is an affront to the grace and faithfulness of God for a Christian believer to ignore God's promised blessings through the atoning work of Christ on the cross and research into past genealogical history looking for curses which were supposed to have been on their ancestors, to identify themselves with such curses, and then turn to a pastor or priest for deliverance from these assumed generational curses.

This is like what the Bible refers to as having "trampled the Son of God underfoot, counted the blood of the covenant by which he was sanctified a common thing, and insulted the Spirit of grace" (Hebrews 10:29).

One songwriter declares: "He [Jesus] came to make His blessings flow as far as the curse is found." And whom God has blessed, no one can curse.

The Bible declares triumphantly: "Blessed be the God and Father of our Lord Jesus Christ, who has blessed us with every spiritual blessing in the heavenly places in Christ" (Ephesians 1:3). *If Christianity fundamentally rests upon belief in the atoning work of Christ on the cross, let us believe in it and gratefully accept its full benefits for all who are true Christian believers.*

There are many whose lives have been bitterly tormented by this superstitious fear of being under a curse. They have had sleepless nights. They are almost nervous wrecks. They add further illness upon themselves to what has been normal ill-health or adversity, just because they have been deceived into thinking they are cursed—that some evil person has brought a curse on them or that they are bearing the curse of their ancestors. Such a deception is nothing but the wiles and lies of the devil seeking to deprive God's children of the glorious awareness of our true blessedness in Christ.

Whom God Has Blessed

❖ *The divine truth is that every believer in Christ is blessed. And whom God has blessed, no one can curse. Amen!*

And so, in closing, I declare to you, dear saints of God, on the authority of the Word of God that in Christ you are blessed by God with all spiritual blessings, whatever your condition or circumstances may be. You do not need any preacher, pastor or priest to remove any generational curse because the generational curse does not exist.

Not even Satan, the father of all evil doers, has the authority or power to inflict evil on God's people without God's permission; and, if God permits him, then the evil he means to inflict will work out for good for God's people. "And we know that God causes all things to work together for good to those who love God, to those who are called according to His purpose" (Romans 8:28).

We thank God that as far as the curse of the Law or the universal curse of sin is concerned, according to the Scriptures, Christ and Christ alone has freed you from this universal curse of sin. Therefore gladly put your trust in Him and accept His redemptive work on your behalf.

Interestingly, having forthrightly rejected the myth of the generational curse doctrine, we may declare the truth of the generational blessing. As was explain in a previous chapter, the generational blessing is, according to the Scriptures, the blessing of the Abrahamic covenant which God has bestowed on all nations in Christ through the redemptive work of Christ on the cross. Therefore you may boldly declare to anyone who tells you of the erroneous idea you are a victim of a curse upon your generations that you are instead rightly more than a conqueror through the blessings of God upon all nations!

We see that through the Abrahamic covenant God promised to bless all the nations of the earth through Abraham's Seed. Jesus Christ became the promised Seed in whom all the nations are blessed (Galatians 3:13-21). Let us who are believers in Christ declare the good news of the generational blessing.

The scriptural declaration of the generational blessing of God upon every believer in Christ through the Abrahamic covenant completely dispels the myth of a generational curse on any of God's children. Let us hold fast our Christian profession. *The divine truth is that every believer in Christ is blessed. And whom God has blessed, no one can curse. Amen!*